Also by Bill Maher

True Story: A Comedy Novel

Does Anybody *have a* Problem *with* That?

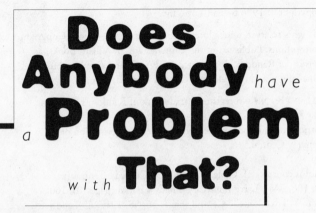

Does Anybody have
a Problem
with That?

Politically Incorrect's
greatest hits

Bill Maher

villard new york

Portions of this book are reproduced by kind permission of
Comedy Central.

Photos courtesy of: Craig Blankenhorn/Comedy Central (pages
70, 106, 244), Larry Busacca/Comedy Central (pages 10, 160),
John W. Fox/Comedy Central (pages 36, 58, 191, 223), and Jeff
Kravitz/Comedy Central (page 202).

ISBN: 0-679-45627-9

Book design by Debbie Glasserman

Printed in the United States of America on acid-free paper
98765432
First Edition

Acknowledgments

Most of the material in this book was "TelePrompTer ready," which means people slaved over the words until they were ready to be actually written out as prose for the prompter (this was in the days of the show when I used to read the questions).

This written material was prepared by the *Politically Incorrect* writing staff, which I proudly count myself among, but I would like to also acknowledge my appreciation to the following folks for not only turning out great stuff for the show, but making me laugh, too: Scott Carter, Christoper Case Erbland, Chris Kelly, Hayes Jackson, Eric Weinberg, John Hotchkiss, and Tim Long.

Contents

Preface

Ever since *Politically Incorrect* went on the air, people have been asking me what the phrase means, and where it puts me politically. The simple answer is that it sounded like a good title, and *Murder, She Wrote* was already taken. The slightly more complicated answer is that the name struck me as a convenient shorthand for my particular take on the world. To me, the notion of politically incorrect is neither liberal nor conservative, but an attitude of disgust toward unthinking, dogmatic politics of every stripe.

In fact, political incorrectness is not really political at all; it's more about not being treated like a child. It's a protest against the view that I am a child whose thoughts need policing, and that no one is capable of acting any better than the stupidest member of our society. For example, I *know* alcoholism is serious, but zillions of people drink and enjoy it and don't become alcoholics, and drunk bits are too funny to throw out of comedy. Trust me, I can tell a Polish joke *and* keep it in my head that Polish people aren't really stupid. Political correctness assumes we're morons who, if allowed to do anything naughty, will immediately turn into unmanageable terrors.

The nineties have been an incorrect time and will continue to be so. They always are. The denouement of a century is frightening, and the onset of a millennium makes you positively shit in your pants. So the nineties are gay, and people don't want to be so good. Smoking is up in America. You can do drug jokes on TV again. Maybe soon we'll be able to hold in our minds *both* concepts about drinking:

that alcoholism is sad, but drunks are funny! Hey, anything could happen, because even *men* are making a comeback, finally coming out of our sulking fit over women demanding the right to be as sleazy in their personal lives and ruthless in their professional ones as we've always been. Around *P.I.* that's what we call an "RBT"—and it's this commitment to stating the "rude but true" that I hope makes this compilation of material from our show stand out. That, and the terrifying, real-life accounts of alien abductions.

I hope you enjoy reading this book as much as I enjoyed having it read to me. And for those who've starting bugging me about when my *next* book will be appearing, be patient: I'm already hard at work on a full behind-the-scenes account of my experience playing the lovable robot C3PO in the popular *Star Wars* film series.

May the Force be with you!

—Bill Maher

Better *to be* Born *with a* Pretty Face *than a* Pointy Head

Are People Getting Stupider?

First aired 10·10·93

Mark Kostabi, Merrill Markoe, John Lawton, Marvin Kitman

SAT scores are plummeting, college graduates can't read, and Americans are paying good money for bell-bottoms again. Let's face it, there *is* an education crisis in this country. In a math and science test among students from fifteen countries last year, the United States came in fourteenth. Slovenia, which has been a country since Tuesday, kicked our ass, and, sadly, literacy scores are no better. Reading, which gave us Shakespeare and Dostoyevsky, is being replaced by a visual culture that so far has made me so sick of seeing Madonna naked that I might as well be married to her. The question is, are people getting stupider, or is it just an impression I have from every second of every day?

• • •

"Is the average person stupider today than he was a generation ago? Or do you just run into more stupid people because fewer stupid people are getting eaten by bears?"
 —Bill

Is America Anti-Intellectual?

First aired 10·29·93

**Jim Morris, Timothy Leary, Sally Kirkland,
Rep. Marjorie Margolies-Mezvinsky**

In America, we often hear the phrase "the best and the brightest," as if we in any remote way consider them to be the same thing. In reality, we always appreciate a president, like Reagan or Bush, who leaves the country a little stupider than he found it, and we never fail to swoon for a smear campaign that labels some poor bastard an egghead, although to be fair, Dwight Eisenhower's "I Like Ike" was just a catchier slogan than Adlai Stevenson's "Smarty Pants for President." It's not that other countries have any more or less intellectuals than we do, it's just that in other places they seem to be admired instead of despised. After America has broken down so many prejudices based on race, sexism, and religion, isn't our bias against brains still the most dangerous of all?

· · ·

"If you don't believe that America is anti-intellectual, then why is it that on Gilligan's Island *the character who had the worst billing was the Professor?"*

—Bill

Beauty Pageants

First aired 2·22·94

Joe Queenan, Jonathan Katz, Janeane Garofalo, Jeffrey Lyons

What with the Miss America pageant just around the corner in September, we thought it appropriate to head off now any of the usual protests that in recent years routinely accompany any beauty pageant—protests that say it's sexist to judge women only on their looks. Hey, the problem with these pageants is that they don't just judge the looks—they throw in a lot of crap about having a talent and answering essay questions—and that America's too sexually repressed, and radical feminists too scary, for us to admit there's nothing wrong with the flagrant flaunting of beauty for beauty's sake. Every category in that pageant should be about beauty: best legs, best smile, best chest of anyone not on *Baywatch*. Does anyone have a problem with that?

• • •

"How is it in this country that, if you pore over that Sports Illustrated *swimsuit issue, you're a pervert, but if you ogle the same babes in alphabetical order by state, you're patriotic?"*
—Bill

• • •

"Beauty pageant women, Sports Illustrated *women, and women who work for Aaron Spelling: They are to me as Uncle*

5

Tom is to the black man. . . . They are such Stepin Fetchit sell-outs."

—Janeane Garofalo

. . .

"We pretend not to tolerate racism on TV and in movies. Yet we allow sexism and objectification to run rampant every day and every way."

—Janeane

"You've said your piece. Let me ask you this: How would you end world hunger?"

—Bill

. . .

"What I think is so dangerous about the beauty pageants is the very narrow scope of what they regard as beautiful. Society in general—its idea of beautiful has much too much to do with thin. My feeling is that when you can actually see a woman digesting, then she's too thin."

—Jonathan Katz

Beauty over Bell Curve

First aired 11·29·94

Chris Rock, Robert B. Parker, Terrie Williams, James Toback

A recent bestseller, *The Bell Curve,* contained the controversial argument that IQ test scores are the most important factor in determining a person's success, although the book was widely criticized for also containing five hundred of Oprah's favorite recipes. Sadly, *The Bell Curve* gets it all wrong: As the O. J. Simpson trial has shown us, it's not brains that are important in life, it's being physically attractive. Stephen Hawking may be a brilliant, groundbreaking physicist, but he makes about one tenth as much as Heather Locklear, even though they're both at the top of their fields and they've both been married to the drummer from Mötley Crüe. You can always get ahead by further educating yourself, but among humans, it just may be better to be born with a pretty face than a pointy head.

• • •

"Money is the great equalizer. Money takes away all your faults. Money will turn a bald spot into a part!"
—Chris Rock

• • •

"You don't hear women described as having rugged good looks."
—James Toback

GET OVER YOURSELVES

Supermodels

First aired 11·2·94

Once again, it's time for our Prince Rogers Nelson "Get Over Yourself" Award, which we give out to the person or persons we feel most in need of getting over themselves.

In honor of Fashion Week here in New York, tonight's award goes to supermodels, who, admittedly through no fault of their own, have been elevated to a status in our society formerly reserved for war heroes and Nobel Prize winners—in other words, people who did something, as opposed to people who just plucked the lucky Pick 6 in the genetic lottery. I don't begrudge Cindy or Niki or Naomi their fame and fortune, because modeling all day is actually hard work. However, if you think it's tough spending all day in a trailer, try living in one. Not to mention how grueling it is cramming into exclusionary restaurants all night and breathing second-hand Mickey Rourke.

No, what I object to is the presumption in every disinterested sneer these girls wear that their stardom is somehow something they had coming to them, when in truth they could have just as easily been born with Down syndrome as with flawless features and long legs. So often we see them acting perturbed and put upon by all the adulation and the burden of being hit on by every man, as if for a second they'd change places with a plainer woman. Life's tough when you have to drink eight glasses of water a day and get paid a lot to, basically, stand there, but when I hear about Claudia Schiffer

8

writing her memoirs at twenty-three, it's almost as if she must have been put under a spell by some magician to think that she belongs in the library next to Schiller and Schopenhauer.

Look, supermodels, it's a short, wild ride, and the same fickle society that can't get enough of you now will get over you soon enough. So, before they do, get over yourselves!

Season One: Too much hair.

The Man who Knew too Much

Is Clinton the Democrats' Reagan?

First aired 10·4·93

**Andrea Martin, Gary Ross,
Tama Janowitz, Tony Snow**

When Ronald Reagan was riding high during his two terms as president, what is it that the Democrats wished for more than anything? They wished that Ronald Reagan was still a Democrat. Like Pepsi and Coke, or Ford and Chrysler, the two political parties don't really care what they make or what they stand for, just so long as they're ahead in market share. Bill Clinton's sudden emergence as a national leader always smelled to me like the result of a Democratic Party planning meeting that began with the words "We've got to find a younger Reagan with a brain." So they looked for another ex-actor, but they found something even better: a talk-show host. Our president is better at their game than Donahue or Oprah, and in being so, isn't Bill Clinton really just the Democrats' Ronald Reagan?

• • •

"If Bill Clinton was Moses, he would have come down with the Ten Suggestions."

—Bill

In Praise of Bill Clinton

First aired 10·29·93

Joe Queenan, Michael O'Donoghue,
Jim Morris, Lynn Martin

Last month, Bill Clinton stepped onstage before a joint session of Congress to deliver the most important address of his life, only to find that the wrong speech had been loaded into the TelePrompTer. And while he masterfully ad-libbed his way through the arcane details of health care, I couldn't help but think what some other presidents would have done in a similar situation: Reagan would've broken into dialogue from *Bedtime for Bonzo,* unless, of course, Nancy was there to cue him; Bush would've thrown up; and Kennedy would've cursed himself for putting that blonde in the steno pool in charge of speeches. Bill Clinton has certainly not been a perfect president, but when it comes to being the smartest kid in the class, being in touch with the people he's governing, tackling problems that his predecessors cowardly swept under the rug for decades, and putting an end to an era that raised selfishness to a virtue—the American people finally got one right when they elected Bill Clinton president of the United States. Has anyone got a problem with that?

• • •

"I picture Clinton late at night after the day's work is done, contemplating infinity. Reagan, on the other hand, I picture late at night trying to guess how many jelly beans are in his jar."
—Bill

The Whitewater Scandal

First aired 3·14·94

**Kelsey Grammer, Cynthia Heimel,
Bruce Herchensohn, Ruth Seymour**

With the Whitewater scandal rising higher all around him, President Clinton stood up, pounded his fist, and called Hillary one of the finest women he's ever had—in his administration, of course. Now, technically she's just a first lady like any other, and running the country isn't something we ever associated with Barbara Bush. Or, for that matter, with George Bush. But in reality, Hillary is a different kind of first lady, and now that she's embroiled in the kind of scandal that we've seen sink so many careers in Washington, the question becomes, will Bill Clinton ask Hillary to step down as his wife, and isn't he already distancing himself from her by seeing other women?

• • •

"With the Whitewater scandal, the question is whether Hillary should do what so many other women have done for the president, and fall on his sword."

—Bill

Should Clinton Twist More Arms?

First aired 10·29·93

Jim Morris, Timothy Leary, Sally Kirkland, Rep. Marjorie Margolies-Mezvinsky

Recently, Janet Reno brought back good memories of strong leadership when she told the entertainment industry to clean up its act or she'd do it for them. And to think she was once this meek little waif who said "please" and "thank you" every time she blew up a building and killed everyone inside. Reno actually reminds me a bit of Lyndon Johnson—okay, she's a little huskier than Johnson—but she really lets you know who's boss. Kind of like Harry Truman, when he stared down the railroad strikers, or JFK when he jawboned the steel barons. Compared with these guys, Mr. Nice Guy Bill Clinton is a nancy boy who hasn't yet learned that twisting elbows and the phrase "Is that a veto in your pocket or are you just glad to see me?" is the way to get things done in Washington. My question is, aren't threats a legitimate part of the arsenal of any effective leader, and shouldn't Clinton start acting like Janet Reno and Hillary and the other women who wear the pants in his administration?

• • •

"Is President Clinton a forceful enough leader? I think most people respect what he says, it's just that every time he laughs after one of his own jokes, I expect that Hee Haw *fence to smack him in the ass."*

—Bill

Politicians Should Steal a Little

First aired 6·24·94

Steve Allen, Lynn Samuels, Christopher Cox, Jonathan Alter

The latest accusations about Hillary Clinton's trading in cattle futures brings up several interesting questions—did she use insider trading to profit, and do slaughterhouse cattle really have a future? But we forget that when Clinton was governor, he made $32,000 a year—back then they *had* to eat at McDonald's. As long as the public cries "foul" when politicians want pay raises—saying in effect that they expect their public servants to be paid, hell, like servants, we are fostering an atmosphere that encourages them to bend the rules. Like policemen, who get paid so little for doing such a big job and feel justified for taking a little graft on the side, can we really blame the politicians for taking advantage of a few perks to even the score, and doesn't part of the blame go to a naive public that expects its leaders to do a CEO's job at a gym teacher's wage?

• • •

"Government pay is so abysmally low, many politicians these days supplement their income by giving talks. For instance, Mario Cuomo makes about $20,000 per speech, Oliver North gets up to $25,000 an hour, and Bob Packwood gets $3.95 a minute."

—Bill

White House Sex Scandals—So What?

First aired 5·6·94

Larry Miller, Joe Queenan, David Brock, Rep. Major Owens

By now we all know that White House sex scandals occur regularly enough to set your alarm clock by—which is probably what Bill does, so he can get home before Hillary wakes up—but the question is, why is that important? When we elected Bill Clinton, we knew what we were getting: a talented politician who took a big bite out of life—all parts of life. In the chess game that is politics, the American people made their move—they chose Bill Clinton—and then they took their hand off the piece, which means it's too late to change their move, and those who continue to whine about President Sex Machine should just shut up.

· · ·

"Remember that 'boxers or briefs' question at the MTV press conference? I think the whole world was shocked that there was a woman in Washington who didn't know what kind of underwear he wore."

—Bill

The President's Real "State of the Union" Speech

First aired 1·25·94

Ladies and gentlemen, members of Congress, members of the press . . . as I look out at all of you, I am once again reminded of an important fact of our civic life: that I do all the work, and you sit there watching me, judging me, perched on your ample, lobby-larded asses, pissed off that I bumped *Roseanne* and somehow trying to imagine in your wildest dreams that you could handle this job for one day without ending up like the nut case in *Full Metal Jacket.* But I digress—now where was I? Oh yeah—screw you. I've chosen that as my new catchphrase; it's a little snappier than "new covenant," and it gets to the heart of my message: I do more before nine A.M. than got done around here in the last twelve years, and you ought to thank your lucky stars you have a president who doesn't fit his work in between naps or pheasant hunting.

First, I got a budget bill passed, which I'd talk about except, quite frankly, it's way too complicated for you to understand, and you don't care, anyway. And speaking of not caring and too complicated, how 'bout getting NAFTA through, all you "visionaries"? God, if this Congress took over a movie studio, they'd call it Nineteenth Century–Fox. Education? Please, the only book you people read is by Howard Stern, so let me know when you want to get serious about that one. Health care? Like everything else, you want all the services, but God forbid you have to pay for something. Grow up: "Tastes great, less filling" is a beer commercial, it's not a model for how life works. Foreign pol-

icy? Yeah, I didn't go to Vietnam, but at least when Bosnia comes up on page twelve, after the Bobbitts and the Menendez kids and the skating stories, I remember *why* I didn't want to go.

I deal with more crap every day than any of you will ever see in your worst nightmares, and all anybody wants to talk about is whether I drove the skin bus with some babe back in Arkansas. Well, as far as my private life goes, you can all blow me down with a feather if you think I'm gonna tell you a damn thing. Remember all that stuff about "I feel your pain"? Well, how 'bout feeling *my* pain for once! All of you . . . you brave, noble citizens of this country. I guess I lost my head there for a minute . . . you know how it is, but the important thing is, we all live in a place called Hope, and in the greatest country in the world, where if we have the courage to change, we can make the future brighter for all of our children. God bless you, and God bless America.

Clinton Should Sleep Around

First aired 8·8·93

So far, Bill Clinton has been a big disappointment to me, and I'm not talking about his politics. No, this is something more fundamental. You see, in Bill Clinton I was sure that we were finally getting a good old-fashioned, screwing-around Kennedy Democrat in the White House—and wouldn't that be better? It would in the eyes of all men out there, if they're honest with themselves.

Because, to us men, the president isn't just the president, he's the tribal chieftain: He's the warrior with the greatest prowess, and the longest spear, and as our chieftain, we look up to him to live beyond the strictures of normal men, as chieftains do. "Bathe her and bring her to my tent"—that's what power is all about. All the men in America didn't agree with John F. Kennedy's politics, but they all respected him as a cocksman. Fittingly, he had his way with the tribe's most desirable maiden, Marilyn Monroe, the only wench truly worthy of the chieftain, and we admired that.

As for Clinton, I think we all had hopes that by now he would have at least gotten Madonna. He seemed to show such a flair for extramarital relations during his run for the White House. Boy, talk about going back on a campaign promise. And please don't think it's the infidelity itself that we admire, but the man is the president, after all, and if he can't get some decent tail, what hope is there for the rest of us? George Bush had a sex scandal during the 1992 cam-

paign with a fifty-eight-year-old woman. Really, George, you were the president, that kind of fooling around is just pathetic, and it certainly didn't win you any votes. Not to mention that many foreign leaders simply won't respect a president who isn't getting something on the side. We look at the world through American eyes, but in Latin America, to say nothing of Italy, if your president doesn't have a scandal, it's a scandal.

I know women don't want to hear this, but isn't it better to face the truth about men than to be constantly disillusioned by them? And the truth is, although women prefer sex when it's loving and intimate and sincere, those things just ruin it for us. We like it when it's dirty, nasty, and just terribly wrong, and that doesn't change just because you're the president—it probably gets worse. The man has the weight of the world on his shoulders; is it so awful once in a while that he ruts like a pig?

Come on, Madonna, if it was good enough for Marilyn Monroe, it's plenty good enough for you. Get over to the White House. Do your patriotic duty.

Which Party Served the Country Better?

First aired 8·29·93

**Larry Miller, Joe Queenan,
Vinette Pryce, Mark Katz**

America is governed—well, sort of—by a two-party system. We elect Democrats to get us goodies, and then we elect Republicans to help us hog them from interlopers and party crashers. There seems a natural rhythm to the two-party system, although sometimes the rhythm method doesn't work, and then we get pregnant with Nixon. Nevertheless, since JFK, Democratic administrations have founded the Great Society and put a man on the moon, and the Republicans have presided over the greatest peacetime weapons expansion ever and the end of the Cold War. My question is, which party since 1960 has served this country best?

• • •

"The two-party system has undergone a lot of changes from Camelot to today, from John F. Kennedy's 'Ask not what your country can do for you . . .' to Teddy Kennedy's 'Let's go someplace quiet.'"

—Bill

Conservative vs. Liberal Convictions

First aired 9·26·93

**Penn Jillette, Norma Ornstein,
Carl Bernstein, Rita Rudner**

If the American government were a restaurant, it would be a different kind of dining experience under Democratic management than it would under Republican management. The Republican restaurant is a diner where the menu never changes. Conservatives know what they want to order when they walk in; they want less social spending and more spending on national defense, so they can honestly tell schoolchildren the government is broke and those grilled cheese sandwiches have to go. The Democratic restaurant, on the other hand, is an upscale, overcrowded yuppie bistro where a well-rehearsed, smiling waiter—that is, the president—is always telling his customers—us—about some specials they have tonight. So our waiter, Bill, has tempted our palates with gays in the military, family leave, spotted owls, war in Bosnia, aid to Russia, a tax on energy, a health care program—and those are only the things his wife is in charge of. My question is, does the fact that conservatives seem to have a much greater conviction in their beliefs make those beliefs more valid?

• • •

"Conservatives know what they want and they never forget it. Except for the time Reagan went to the Vietnam Memorial and shouted, 'Mr. Gorbachev, tear down this wall!'"
 —Bill

Redemption Politics

First aired 10·20·94

**Floyd Brown, Linda Doucett,
Mykel Board, Rolonda Watts**

These days, there's something truly remarkable happening in American politics, and I'm not talking about Dan Quayle writing a book. Or even reading one. Politicians were once guys who never thought about committing a crime—well, at least until they got into office. But these days, if you're trying to get elected, it actually pays to be a lawbreaker. Take Ollie North and Marion Barry, two candidates with little in common except their criminal records and, surprisingly, a taste for early Earth, Wind & Fire. Which brings me to the following question: In the law, on Wall Street, and even in baseball, one transgression gets you tossed out for life, so why are Pete Rose and Michael Milken held to a higher standard than our elected politicians?

• • •

"These days, Jeffrey Dahmer could run for office. His slogan would be, 'I'll take a bite out of crime.'"
—Bill

Let 'Em See You Sweat

First aired 9·26·93

"Never let 'em see you sweat" is the sort of folk wisdom that gets created on Madison Avenue and then waved on through into popular belief without any thought as to whether or not it's true. I know of at least two places where it's not true, and that's show business and politics—although that's really one place.

In fact, one piece of evidence that politics is just show business for ugly people is that in both professions—and I use that word loosely—people very definitely *do* want to see you sweat. Whether it's the spectacle of million-dollar athletes breaking down in the locker room from media pressure, or politicians forgoing all dignity while flipping burgers or milking cows for votes, or movie stars airing out in public a raft of embarrassing tragedies and addictions—the dirty secret of show business is that the audience loves to see its idols suffer.

Take Bill Clinton. He got to the White House by eating the shiitake mushrooms that the voters demand as the penance for being young, powerful, and getting more nooky on the side than they are. We smelled success on Clinton, but before he became Heap Big Chief we wanted him to walk through the standard gauntlet that our tribe uses to pick a president: sex scandals, *60 Minutes,* drugs, draft dodging—the usual suspects—and it wasn't in spite of these

scandals that Clinton got elected, it was *because* of them, because he knew how to handle them.

That's what the game is all about—how you handle your beating. The American people want to see you smile while you take your whipping, boy, they don't want no Bob Dole bitching about it, or Ed Muskie crying about it, or Gary Hart lying about it. They just want to see you sweat. Just like the people in Las Vegas want to see Wayne Newton go through twenty silk scarves, or watch James Brown wear out a drummer.

Elvis Presley in his bloated years was more beloved than ever because Elvis's misery confirmed our secret hope that being so extraordinary is nothing to be wished for. "Good thing I wasn't born Elvis," we could say, "look what happened to him." Yeah, it did happen to him, but I'll give you my hunch: It was worth it.

Political Coattails

First aired 10·25·94

**Paul Rudnick, Rep. Major Owens,
LeVar Burton, Cathy Ladman**

Political endorsements were a big item in the news this week—yesterday, here in New York, Mayor Rudolph Giuliani crossed party lines to endorse Mario Cuomo; and out in California, the normally reticent Clint Eastwood asked voters to make his Tuesday by rejecting the Manchurian Candidate, Michael Huffington, in favor of Democrat Dianne Feinstein. A fundamental question about all this is "Why?"—and not only "Why?" but "Who?"—as in "Who cares?" Who cares about what is basically a glorified letter of recommendation from someone who we often don't even respect to begin with? Or, if we do, certainly not enough to follow in lockstep into the voting booth. I mean, if you find out that Keanu Reeves is "a Clinton dude, man," is that really enough to sway your vote? And, if it is, check out the acting in *Dracula* again—Bob Dole might start to look a little better. My question is, does it matter when actors endorse politicians, and, if so, why?

Richard Nixon

First aired 4·29·94

**Martin Mull, Frank Gannon,
Ruth Shalit, Ken Hamblin**

The moving spectacle of Richard Nixon's funeral made one thing clear: In death, Richard Nixon was able to do what he wasn't able to do in life—really shut down the government.

It is a testament to the true generosity of spirit that characterizes Americans that, this past week, we've all given up accuracy and perspective to eulogize a man for the virtues he did have: Nixon was smart, he was effective in getting things done in government before he was crippled, he knew how to deal with our enemies, and he was right—that is the president's first job.

His problem was, he dealt with American "enemies" the same way. He was that rare thing in politics, a true good family man; but outside of that, he was a shrewd, calculating, ruthless son of a bitch. Which is just the kind of guy you want to have dealing with America's enemies. But Democrats and the press within America are not the enemy, they're adversaries.

Nixon's greatest legacy will prove to be the cynicism America now has for its government. Of all his virtues recounted this week, the one that stood above the rest was that Nixon never quit; he never fell to his knees. But while he was standing throughout Watergate, the country was on its knees, the stock market fell, and that volatile world out there he had done so much to make safer was pissing its pants. Never quitting can be a very selfish thing. My question is, Richard Nixon: Where is he right now, heaven or hell?

• • •

"Everyone paid tribute to Nixon this week. Reagan was particularly eloquent—he said he'd miss his friend, his great mind, his sage advice, but that he was sure he'd come back. Then he realized he was thinking about the death of Spock."
—Bill

• • •

"I know where he is now, but I've been sworn to secrecy."
—Frank Gannon

• • •

"I understand he thought ahead and had his casket bugged."
—Bill

• • •

"He was probably one of the more well-traveled presidents . . . and I would think after some seventy years of travel, of being on the road, living out of a suitcase, I would say he would go to whichever is closer to Yorba Linda. And being from the state of California, I just hope he brought his suntan oil."
—Martin Mull

• • •

"Didn't he abolish caning?"
—Martin

GET OVER YOURSELF

Newt Gingrich

First aired 11·18·94

Well, it's time once again for our Prince Rogers Nelson "Get Over Yourself" Award. Tonight, the award goes to a man who has pride in the Senate and an ego the size of the House. Newt Gingrich is a politician who is fast making many of us who might otherwise agree with some of his goals take the other side just because he is so personally obnoxious. Reaganism needed its founder's kindly face and kindly qualities; coming out of the mouth of a strutting, conceited pug it sounds mean and scary. Not that Reagan would say anything as stupid—even now—and un-American as Gingrich's rant connecting mothers who drown babies and voting for Democrats. Newt also mentioned in passing recently that if you voted against his ideas, you were not a normal American. Hey, if he's normal, pass the sitar.

It's good to have strong convictions, of course, but when the people you disagree with are enemies and not normal, that sounds more like the kind of thing Americans have given their lives, over the years, to stamping out. This guy has got to get over himself: The day after elections, he took an hour and a half to return a call from the president—and even then put him on speakerphone. But perhaps the worst is Gingrich's plan to have his "Contract with America" read every morning in Congress for the first one hundred days—like these guys don't have enough trouble staying awake. They don't read the Declaration of Independence, or the

Emancipation Proclamation—but now we have to pray every day from the Book of Newt?

Hey, make all the Ted Kennedy drinking jokes you want, it's being drunk with power that is the real danger in politics. So, Newt, from the counterculture to the culture counter: Get over yourself, buddy!

Countries *that* **Love** *too much,* *and the* **Starving** **Masses** *that* **Hate** *them*

*Lorraine Bracco, Matt Lauer, Roseanne, John O'Sullivan:
Somebody here had 21 personalities that day.*

Moral America

First aired 9·19·93

**Roseanne, Matt Lauer, Lorraine Bracco,
John O'Sullivan**

The fifty-year bar brawl this country had with Russia ended with the collapse of the Soviet Union, and now America sits astride the world unchallenged like no power since ancient Rome. When Romans had that kind of power, they lived by the famous rubric "If you can't eat it, sell it, or screw it—kill it," but America does not do her business that way. For example, when Vietnam had a civil war, we sent our troops, but when we had our civil war, there wasn't one Vietnamese soldier over here helping. The point is, America could bully the world and make the Idi Amin regime look like a tea party in Murray Hill, but we don't, and we should get credit for that. Does anyone have a problem with that?

• • •

"America is the only country in the world that's still in the business of making bombs that can end the world and TV shows that make it seem like a good idea."
 —Bill

For Political Asylum, You Must Plot

Steve Allen, Lynn Samuels, Rep. Christopher Cox, Jonathan Alter

Every week, thousands of foreign nationals pass under the welcoming armpit of the Statue of Liberty, and when they ask for political asylum, they're basically saying, "Things suck so bad in my country that I actually prefer living in New York." The problem is, there's crushing political repression in dozens of countries, and for all the oppressed people around the world to simply turn their backs on their fellow nationals and take up life in America isn't the right answer for them or us. Of course, that doesn't mean America shouldn't help, but I say that if you are here as a victim of political repression, then while in America you must get together with the other repressed people from your country and plot the overthrow of your nation's government—not our government, World Trade Center bombers; *your* government can't have a free ride forever. In other words, you can have political asylum, but you *must plot.*

• • •

"A lot of Americans don't think it's right that there are so many illegal immigrants roaming the countryside in rags and not paying taxes, because that's Willie Nelson's job."

—Bill

Caning

First aired 4·8·94

**Sen. Arlen Specter, Gloria Allred,
John Waters, Sarah Jessica Parker**

In the last few years, many people have called for stiffer laws against graffiti, although here in New York, school officials say it has led to improved literacy rates. But in some places around the world, the upholding of civilization is still taken seriously, so much so that an American youth in Singapore who was caught after a weeklong spree of vandalism has been sentenced to six whacks with a four-foot water-soaked wicker and rattan cane, which is available at Pier 1 Imports. The fact is, public flaying is an accepted form of justice in Singapore, whereas here in New York that type of behavior is usually considered performance art, which brings up two questions: Should the U.S. government intervene, and how bad of an artist must this kid be? I say that if you want to commit a crime and go unpunished, stay in America. But when in Rome, if you spray-paint the Vatican, don't come crying to your Uncle Sam.

• • •

"Michael Fay's parents have asked the Red Cross to oversee the caning, where the young boy will be stripped naked and have his bare buttocks beaten raw with a wet cane. If the Red Cross can't make it, several thousand Catholic priests have offered to fill in."

—Bill

• • •

"I'm against caning, unless two people do it for fun at home."
—John Waters

American Foreign Legion

First aired 4·22·94

**Charles Peters, Maureen Reagan,
Michael Moriarty, Peter Fonda**

In this complicated, post–Cold War world, it's not so easy anymore to put a face on evil—although Burt Reynolds comes pretty close. So when trouble erupts in Bosnia or Haiti—or any other country that's on CNN more than Larry King—we're torn between our humanitarian wish to right a wrong and our reluctance to risk even one good man or woman. Which brings up the question, what about risking a bad one? The idea of using downtrodden ne'er-do-wells with nothing left to lose—prisoners, criminals, misfits—has already been proven to work, and I'm not talking about the Rose law firm. I'm talking about the French Foreign Legion. Giving a man who's used up all his chances one more chance to redeem himself by serving his country could alleviate both our overcrowded prisons and our schizophrenia about sending Americans into battle around the world. The American Foreign Legion—why not give it a try?

• • •

"Right on the front page, we read about more violence and more bloodshed and more fighting. And now Tom and Roseanne say they're reconciling."

—Bill

Vietnam: Noble, Smart War

First aired 11·26·93

**Ben Stein, Mo Gaffney, Lisa Sliwa,
Christopher Matthews**

In the 1960s, it was often said about Vietnam, "It's a dirty, ugly, nasty war, but be thankful it's the only one we've got." But that wasn't quite true: Vietnam was really part of a global war fought in small representative skirmishes between the United States and Russia. The Cold War wasn't cold for millions of people—it's just that the hot battles were fought far from the warring countries' own territory. There was no home-court advantage in the Cold War, and Vietnam, like other flash points, was a test of will between East and West. If the war hadn't been in Vietnam, it would have been somewhere closer, and that's why Vietnam was not just a noble war, but a smart war to have fought. Does anyone have a problem with that?

• • •

"Vietnam was a war that tore this country apart. Of course, that's nothing compared to what this country did to Vietnam."

• • •

"When we protested the war at Kent State, four people died and in about three days we had disco. History proves that when things get rough, dance crazes come back. Khrushchev killed the twist."

—Bill

China—Human Rights / Wrongs

First aired 3·15·94

**Arianna Huffington, Tim Allen,
Ed Asner, Tom Hayden**

When it comes to human rights, the Chinese have a checkered past. From the annexing of Tibet to the massacre in Tiananmen Square, to pissing off Richard Gere on a daily basis, the leadership of China has continued to stick a thumb in America's eye, and not even the satin-smooth charm and brutal sex appeal of Warren Christopher has been able to make the Chinese cry "Uncle Sam." After all their promises about reform, to both Republican and Democrat administrations, the question still remains: Will the Chinese deliver, and how long will it take to get there?

• • •

"China has a terrible human rights record and they're still Communist. Instead of courting them, I think we should be isolating them. There's an idea: Why don't we just build a huge wall around China?"

—Bill

• • •

"The Chinese can rewrite history. They have a different calendar: It's a rat one year and a cow the next. According to their calendar, they won World War II."

—Tim Allen

A MODEST PROPOSAL

Make Communism Performance Art

1 0 · 2 2 · 9 3

For anyone who loves having a good enemy in their life, the collapse of the Soviet Union has been the most disastrous foreign policy event since the public emptying of Fawn Hall's panties. It's always easier for any nation to identify itself in terms of an enemy, to say the Russians are this and we're that; they're bad, we're good; they're mean, we're nice; they're imprisoned, we're free; they're drunks, we're . . . recovering alcoholics.

So since 1989, we've been hunting around for a new enemy, and for a while it seemed that Saddam Hussein was our man. We convinced ourselves his "fourth largest army in the world" could fill the boots left behind by the retreating Evil Empire, but once his emancipated troops were driven from hiding and revealed that they had in fact eaten their shoes, we began looking elsewhere. We went to Somalia because we thought maybe we could redefine our army as a kind of really kick-ass Red Cross, but after we flew halfway around the world to deliver food, Somalia didn't even tip. So screw them.

No, there's nothing like good old Communism, and let's face it, without Commies to hunt, James Bond is just another horny guy with a compass watch. The obvious solution to this crisis is to bankroll the USSR back into existence. So why did Soviet Communism fall? Because the

Russians can only do two things well—drink and write. Picture a nation of Dylan Thomases and Charles Bukowskis—half of them women. Now imagine them all standing in line for six hours waiting to buy an egg, and you realize it's a miracle they lasted this long.

We rescued Chrysler and look at the results—some of the finest car commercials this nation has ever produced. And where would the American farmer be without a little help every fiscal quarter or so? In other words, just because a system can't survive on its own is no reason to let it perish. But these things take a little bureaucratic end-running, so I say it's time to declare Communism an enormous performance art piece and have it endowed by the NEA. At the very least, we could give them a MacArthur "genius" fellowship. If the "avant-garde" clown Bill Irwin can get one, why not the nation that produced Solzhenitsyn?

Our Criteria for Invasion

First aired 9·5·93

**Joy Behar, Moon Zappa,
Jay Severin, Sy Sperling**

During the Gulf War, some suggested that we should bomb Iraq back to the Stone Age, which sounded like a good idea until it was pointed out that this would only set Iraqis back about three weeks. It's time we admitted that, since Vietnam, we've only fought the easier countries—Iraq, Panama, Grenada—and if this were the World Boxing Federation, we'd be fined for not taking on a contender. To use a more familiar analogy, we *are* the policeman of the world, but like many policemen, we seem quick to respond only in wealthy neighborhoods. As Bosnia now stands in such contrast to Kuwait, the question is, what should be, and what really are, our criteria for an invasion?

• • •

"Our criterion for invading other countries is usually oil, whether it's Kuwait, Libya, or the Branch Davidian compound. Why do you think it burned so fast?"
 —Bill

Saddam Hussein's "Intervention"

First aired 10·19·94

**Joe Queenan, Harry Smith,
E. Jean Carroll, Joe Bolster**

Well, President Clinton has looked like a foreign policy genius lately by threatening intervention first in Haiti and then in Iraq. "Intervention" is the word presidents use when they want to scare a dictator out of office, but for some dictators, like Saddam Hussein, it just doesn't seem to make them go. That's why I suggest that the next time Saddam acts up, instead of a military intervention, we try the other kind of intervention, the kind AA uses. I say we get all of Saddam Hussein's friends together, like at an OPEC meeting, and then when he walks in, we hit him with the truth:

"Saddam—you're a dictator, man. And we want you to know that you have a deadly enemy and it's not the UN. It's you. Oh, yes—you're in denial. Just because you don't want Kuwait to be there won't make it go away. You're not fooling anybody by massing troops on the border. We've seen that trick—and it *is* a trick. You're not being honest with yourself. Somewhere inside you, you know you really don't have the fourth-largest army in the world—Finland could beat you, and I know that's cruel, but I don't want to see you end up like so many other good . . . bloodthirsty tyrants. Your ego is writing checks the Republican Guard can't cash. Yes, you have the power to cut off people's hands, but when you do they can't clap for you, so who are you really hurting? Look, when you drop poison gas on someone, to them

it reads, "Hey, he's pushing me away." That's negative. Let me tell you something—the most potent biological weapon I know is the human heart. There's no embargo on our love and affection, my friend. Give my love to your wives, and death to all Jews."

Democracy | Inaction

Anti–Motor Voter

First aired 10·17·93

**Ben Stein, Mo Gaffney,
Jill Brooke, Christopher Hitchens**

The Motor Voter Bill now requires states to allow registration wherever people get a driver's license, enlist in the military, collect unemployment, and go on welfare. I guess voting and a McDonald's giveaway is not too far off—get a Big Mac and register, and the Pepsi's free. My question is, why are we always begging people to vote? It's embarrassing. The people in this country are the luckiest people on earth; if they don't realize it, screw them. On the contrary: We should be grateful that the disinterested and brain dead know who they are and at least have the good taste to stay home on Election Day. Anybody got a problem with that?

• • •

"Democrats in the Senate have been for the Motor Voter Bill, Republicans against it, and Jesse Helms is abstaining until someone explains the invention of the automobile."
 —Bill

Sitcoms = Democracy

First aired 7·25·93

**Larry Miller, Jerry Seinfeld,
Robin Quivers, Ed Rollins**

Last month, Senator Paul Simon scolded Hollywood for producing too much sex and violence—and at such high prices, too. Simon says that we're being force-fed serial killings and car chases, when what we really want is *Masterpiece Theatre*. This guy is either full of shiitake mushrooms, or his bow tie is too tight. We get exactly the entertainment we deserve, the same as we get exactly the political leadership we deserve. Whether it's test audiences, sneak previews, and TV ratings, or focus groups, primaries, and political polls, the powers that be have gotten the science of monitoring our precise desires down to, well, a science. So the place to find blame for the quality of our leadership and the quality of television—present company excepted—is the mirror.

• • •

"In focus groups, they ask a hundred people in a mall to make judgments for millions, who then have to live with Michael Dukakis and arena football."

—Bill

American Royalty

Air date 11·19·93

Joy Behar, Fab 5 Freddy, Gay Talese, Paul Rudnick

Bulimics, toe-suckers, wiretappers, and men who want to be reincarnated as Tampax. Fodder for the next *Geraldo*? No, just a reunion among the British royal family, who lately have been working overtime at—well, not at actually working, of course, since that might involve paying taxes—but at proving that centuries of cousins marrying cousins really can take a toll. And yet, even with that poor example, we Americans continue to yearn for our own royalty, as evidenced by the regal presence in our lives of such noble personages as Lady Schick, Lady Remington, and, of course, Lady Clairol. The point is, royalty does serve a purpose by deflecting scandal away from a nation's government—you never hear about Prime Minister Major wanting to live in someone's trousers. So isn't it time our scandal-ridden government gave it a chance?

• • •

"The royal family—you can't live with them, and the Irish can't seem to blow them up."

—Bill

Bring Back the Smoke-Filled Room

First aired 12·12·93

**Harry Shearer, Fran Drescher,
Eugene McCarthy, Rep. Bernie Sanders**

In America, we're so proud of giving voice to the common man that we seem to need a vote for everything: who's best and worst dressed, which Elvis to put on a stamp, who wins the geek on *Love Connection*. But when it really comes to picking geeks, nothing beats the system of primaries by which we have come to select our parties' candidates in the last twenty years. New Hampshire and Iowa have become all-powerful kingmakers—which is really frightening, because these are places that just got disco. Since the advent of primary primacy, we have been given candidates like Michael Dukakis, Walter Mondale, and George Bush, whereas the old smoke-filled room gave us men like Truman, Eisenhower, and Kennedy. I say, put the old professionals back in charge of politics. Does anyone have a problem with that?

. . .

"The American political process: Every four years, candidates running for president put together educated position papers, announce detailed policy changes, hire Ivy League advisors—and then go to Iowa to suck up to farmers."

—Bill

Vote of No Confidence

First aired 4·8·94

Sen. Arlen Specter, Gloria Allred, John Waters, Sarah Jessica Parker

As President Clinton travels around the country this week, selling solutions to the problems Americans elected him to solve, the taint of scandal continues to dog him at every turn. Which shouldn't surprise anyone, given that his Secret Service code name is "Wet Spot." We've seen it before—an institutionalized media and congressional hysteria that paralyzes our leaders, like it did with Watergate, Iran-Contra, and, most tragically, the recent Buttmaster fiasco over at *Arsenio.* Rather than suffer this daily spectacle of revelations, other democracies, like Britain, have a solution; it's called a vote of no confidence—in one roll call, they either reaffirm their commitment to a weary leader or go with someone else. Since we here in America can't seem to break our addiction to the seedy and the lurid, why not adopt this system?

· · ·

"This week, investigators found that not only did Clinton use his influence to get a $300,000 government loan, he also never returned his neighbor's Weed-Whacker."

—Bill

The **Best Things** *in* **Life Aren't Free**

*Penn Jillette, Michael Elliot, Fran Lebowitz, Henry Rollins: This is the Dirty Dozen
panel of misfits I'd take on a raid against the Nazis.*

Social Clubs

First aired 10·4·93

**Penn Jillette, Michael Elliot,
Fran Lebowitz, Henry Rollins**

Folk wisdom says that opposites attract, but that doesn't hold true for social endeavors, where people generally seek out their own kind. Veterans socialize with other vets at the local VFW; black college students choose to sit with other black students in college cafeterias; and men wearing loud, multicolored plaid pants are either together on the golf course or together on *Soul Train*. If this type of association by choice—which by definition excludes some others—is natural to all groups, why all the fuss about "exclusivity" in social clubs? Doesn't the government have anything better to do than worry about who you hang out with?

● ● ●

"Woody Allen used to talk about never joining a club that would have him as a member. Who knew then that he was talking about the PTA?"

—Bill

Heidi Fleiss and Jack Kevorkian

First aired 11·5·93

Dom Irrera, David Kennerly, Cynthia McFadden, Don Novello

This month, two visionaries of American social life will stand trial for the crime of being ahead of their time. I'm talking about Heidi Fleiss and Dr. Kevorkian—the queen and the king of coming and going. Their homes have been labeled crime scenes, but why is it a crime to put someone out of his misery? And Kevorkian provides a good service too. In a generation or two, when America grows up and finally sheds its puritanical repressions, Americans will erect statues to these enablers of sex and death, and these erections will remind us of Heidi and Dr. Kevorkian and what pioneers they truly were. Anybody got a problem with that?

· · ·

"Rumor is, Heidi Fleiss and Dr. Kevorkian are actually joining forces and have come up with a machine for people who want to kill themselves because they can't get laid."
—Bill

Flag Burning

First aired 12·19·93

**Larry Miller, Phyllis Hyman,
Letitia Baldrige, Joe Conason**

Flag burning is the great litmus test of the right to free speech. It tests it because it's such an emotional issue; in fact, an obscure politician in the Republican Party named George Bush actually got elected president in 1988 defending the flag against the otherwise "perfect" candidate, Michael Dukakis—proving what a potent hold on the American heart does this piece of cloth retain. The question is, when you burn a flag, are you a patriot or a traitor?

• • •

"Flag burning is truly bipartisan—what other political act annoys veterans and damages the ozone layer at the same time?"
—Bill

Lenin as Icon

First aired 10·22·93

**Vladimir Pozner, Emily Prager,
Bob Somerby, Joe Walsh**

In Russia, the body of Communism's most powerful icon, Vladimir Lenin, has been lying inside a mausoleum in Red Square since 1924—which is odd, since Lenin died in 1937. Anyway, now the great Russian people face a seminal decision: whether to keep Lenin where he is or to finally bury him. Or, perhaps as a compromise, to sell him to Michael Jackson. We may laugh at this dilemma in America, but the truth is, we have a similar problem with our own Confederate flag—like Lenin, the symbol of a fallen regime that many still revere. But I say, if you lost the war, take your losers' flags and your dead bodies and bury them so that everyone can start living in the present. Does anyone have a problem with that?

Free Speech Is Our
Most Hated Speech

First aired 6·10·93

**Penn Jillette, Norman Ornstein,
Carl Bernstein, Rita Rudner**

One issue that seems to come up over and over again these days in America is what to do about hate-mongering speech that incites riots and appeals to the most vile, primitive biases within us. One answer is, just don't watch *Love Connection.* But there are those who would take this further, among them a group that wants to adopt a similar law to the one France now has prohibiting any writing that questions the existence of the Holocaust. That position is, of course, abhorrent, but what about the people in America who think that professional wrestling is real? A country that bans the questioning of one thing might someday be a country where you can get fined for saying that wrestling's fixed—it is, by the way. But I don't want to lose the freedom to say that, and so I'm saying that without hate speech, some people wouldn't share at all, and that being able to say the worst things is what America is all about. Does anyone have a problem with that?

• • •

"Free speech, if you include phone sex, can cost up to $4.99 a minute."

—Bill

The Obscenity Police

First aired 9·5·93

**Joy Behar, Moon Zappa,
Jay Severin, Sy Sperling**

Supreme Court Justice Potter Stewart once said that he could not define obscenity, but he knew it when he saw it. Hey, Mr. Justice, stop with all your technical legalese. Knew it when he saw it, that's it? In other words, we have laws based on what one old white guy thinks is dirty. But given that Justice Stewart and most of his colleagues grew up at a time when the word "damn" uttered in *Gone With the Wind* was scandalous, and given the fact that today most kindergarteners are as likely to flip you off as a marine, and that daytime soaps are hotter than anything in the movies—why even try to define obscenity? Shouldn't we just junk the FCC?

• • •

"Do we really need the FCC? It's a giant federal regulatory bureaucracy, and it couldn't even protect us from Dr. Quinn, Medicine Woman.*"*

—Bill

Salman Rushdie |

First aired 2·4·94

**Al Franken, Rep. Bernie Sanders,
Paul Weyrich, Jane Wallace**

In 1988, Salman Rushdie published *The Satanic Verses,*
which prompted the Ayatollah Khomeini to demand his
head on a stake—which, even in Iran, is considered a bad
review. Since that time, Rushdie has been critical of Western
governments for not ostracizing Iran on his behalf, but if
you read between the diplomatic lines, the message from
Washington and London is this: Iran is too strategic a
nation for our relations with it to be based on the plight of
one man, no matter how just his cause may be. My question
is this: Should the U.S. government cast its protective net
around Rushdie, or should we let this Salman swim up-
stream alone?

• • •

*"The sad fact is, we live in a world where mere words put to
paper can make someone want to kill the author. Here in
America, we thought we were safe from that kind of thing—
until they put out* The Bridges of Madison County.*"*
 —Bill

Gangster Rappers

First aired 3·16·94

**Dick Clark, Corbin Bernsen,
Quentin Tarantino, Margaret Smith**

Rap records have, in recent years, forced this nation to ask itself two important questions: Do violent lyrics incite violent actions? and Where's the melody? The so-called gangsta rappers sing about guns and they fire guns—and it's nice to see for once a celebrity actually using the product he endorses. Nevertheless, rap should not be censored, because rap is today's rock and roll, meaning it's the music that scares your parents, and that's what rock and roll is supposed to do—alert the older generation to the anger of the younger. Does anybody have a problem with that?

• • •

"If Mozart were alive today, he'd still be too young to join the Traveling Wilburys."

—Bill

• • •

"When they say, kill a cop, whatever, they hate the police, all right. I've lived in Los Angeles my whole life and the LAPD is a bunch of brownshirts, man."

—Quentin Tarantino

Packwood Diaries

First aired 10·29·93

**Joe Queenan, Michael O'Donoghue,
Jim Morris, Lynn Martin**

This past week, Robert Packwood—senator, author, and lover—was subpoenaed by the Senate Ethics Committee to hand over his personal diary. Packwood responded by saying that he preferred to keep his log to himself, but apparently it's a little late for that. The senator's next tactic was to point out that his diary contains a wide variety of unsavory information, such as other senators' sexual exploits, tales of drunkenness by party officials, and a lurid description of how they make Slim Jims. But no matter what may be in these writings, the point is, a diary is a place for private reflection, soul searching, and a short list of who likes leather. And if government can demand on-site inspection of someone's most personal thoughts, how long will it be before every personal journal begins: "Dear Diary: Can't talk now. Big Brother's watching."

• • •

"The Packwood diaries must be pretty racy, because most of the people who read them apparently cannot wait to get to the bottom of the next page. Which, of course, was Packwood's problem, too."

—Bill

Loitering Laws

First aired 8·22·93

**Michael Medved, Lisa Sliwa,
Sean Kelly, Joe Franklin**

Recently, in the quiet, residential neighborhood where I used to live in Los Angeles, there suddenly was a problem with prostitutes hanging out on the corner. Naturally, I was outraged, so I complained to the police. I said, "Do you have any idea what these girls are charging?" Unfortunately, the police didn't hear me, because I had that newspaper in front of my face. But where is it written that prostitutes—or beggars, or threatening gangs of ruffians—have the right to congregate wherever they want? The card-carrying members of the ACLU would have you believe that the Constitution guarantees freedom of assembly—even for hooligans. But those limousine liberals probably never have to walk down Scary Street, USA, for a quart of milk. Basketball has the three-second rule, how about the three-minute rule for our streets: Over three minutes in one place on the sidewalk, and you're under arrest for loitering! Anybody have a problem with that?

• • •

"Time was when a cop would come along and move people off a street corner; now we rely on drive-by shootings."
—Bill

Limousine Liberals

First aired 4·15·94

**William Kunstler, Steve Allen,
Brett Butler, Donovan Leitch**

In an effort to fight gang warfare, Americans have tried just about everything, including gun control, hiring more cops, and asking gang members to refer to themselves as the Sharks and the Jets. Recently, five thousand residents of a Chicago housing project asked the police to conduct warrantless gun searches in their development. The police were happy to comply—mostly because the last search netted $35 in sofa change—but they never got the chance, because before you could say "limousine liberal," the ACLU filed a lawsuit arguing that such gun sweeps violate the Fourth Amendment. The ACLU as usual may have its heart in the right place, but the reality is they're protecting criminals at the expense of law-abiding citizens—and that's the Mafia's job! Now, the Fourth Amendment, like freedom of speech or *Matlock,* is a cornerstone of the American legal system, but if people want to trade certain rights to make their lives safer, why should the ACLU, or anyone else, stop them?

• • •

"Just last week, over a seventy-two-hour period, gang members in Chicago exchanged hundreds of shots. Which was tragic not only because it wounded five innocent bystanders, but it also gave an entire block the mistaken impression that the Bulls had won a championship."

—Bill

We never have two comics on one panel, but we made an exception for two great old friends, Jerry Seinfeld and Larry Miller.

Police State

First aired 9·12·93

**Curtis Sliwa, Larry Miller, Jerry Seinfeld,
Dr. Wilbert A. Tatum**

Remember when Los Angeles girded itself before the second Rodney King verdict by putting more cops on the street? Guess what? For the first time in years, nobody got murdered. Crime went down. The same thing happens during the Olympics, or anytime the president comes to town or, even more secure, Sinatra. And if Frank Sinatra *and* the president come to town at the same time, not only does the city get safer, but the hookers get way better-looking. I don't know if that's for the president or Sinatra—but I never bet against Frank. The goal of a democracy is to have each of its citizens treated like Frank Sinatra, and if more cops around make things work better, what's so bad about a little bit of a police state?

. . .

"Policemen . . . it's always the same, isn't it? They're never around when you need one, but the second you stab someone in the throat . . ."

—Bill

Twelve *really* Stupid Angry men

Jury Duty

First aired 10·24·93

**Rep. Susan Molinari, Jim Glassman,
Rob Nelson, Dr. Dre**

When the jury system was created in medieval England, the goal of finding twelve peers so unbiased as to have no prior knowledge of the trial they were judging was easily achievable because there were no such things as TVs, newspapers, or camcorders. The problem is, we have all those things today, and we're still trying to find people to sit on a jury who are completely ignorant of highly publicized cases. For example, one of the jurors at the second Rodney King trial had never seen the video! By sticking to this anachronistic system, aren't we ensuring a trial by twelve of our stupidest peers?

• • •

"As the old folk wisdom goes, do you really want to have your fate determined by twelve people who couldn't get out of jury duty?"

—Bill

The Modern Scarlet Letter

First aired 7·25·93

**Larry Miller, Jerry Seinfeld,
Robin Quivers, Ed Rollins**

Mankind has a long history of branding evildoers, starting with God marking Cain after the death of Abel, right through to Colonial New England, where they slapped a scarlet letter on your chest if you were guilty of illicit sex. Of course, nowadays if you have dangerous sex, they put an AIDS ribbon on your chest and you get to go to the Oscars. But other transgressors are not so lucky. In some communities, drunken drivers have to carry stickers on their cars, and sex offenders have been made to place a sign on their front yard advertising their perversity. Worst of all, some towns have taken to publishing the names of johns when they're arrested with a hooker. The question is, does society have the right to rip the newspaper we're holding in front of our face away from us and punish our crimes with our very privacy?

Lawyers

First aired 8·29·93

**Larry Miller, Joe Queenan,
Vinette Pryce, Mark Katz**

In 1965, the Catholic Church stopped insisting that the mass be said in Latin. Many to this day feel that this was a big mistake, since churchgoers could now actually understand what was going on, and so found themselves saying things like "Mary was a *what* when she gave birth to Jesus?" Lawyers never made that same mistake with Latin, and every time one of us doesn't know what a *quid pro quo* is or what *caveat emptor* means, we pay through the nose. If a priesthood can be described as a small cabal who make themselves indispensable by secreting unto themselves the rubrics of the tribe, have we not created a priesthood of lawyers in America?

• • •

"Lawyers are now being used in laboratory experiments in place of white mice, so that the scientists who work in the lab don't become too attached."

• • •

"There is one company in America that does business without lawyers—the Mafia."

—Bill

77

Hate Crimes

First aired 1·7·94

**Al Franken, Alan Dershowitz,
Maureen O'Boyle, Armstrong Williams**

If the opposite of hate is love, what is the opposite of a hate crime? Someone getting assaulted out of fondness? To my knowledge, there has never been a humanitarian at a cross burning—unless, of course, it's the guest of honor. Still, the Supreme Court says hate crimes deserve stiffer penalties, as if when you get stabbed in the neck, the wound is somehow deeper if it came about because you're black or white or Muslim or wear dreadlocks or think Bette Midler is fabulous. It's as if they're saying "A sick mind is a terrible thing to waste"—we really ought to find out more about it. Well, I've got an idea: How about we just lock it up and assume all senseless violence is—what's the word?—senseless. Does anyone have a problem with that?

• • •

"Prosecuting hate crimes is like asking judges to be reading criminals' minds. The problem is, I don't know, a couple of Supreme Court judges just retired because they were having trouble reading their own mail."

—Bill

The Denny Verdict

First aired 10·22·93

Vladimir Pozner, Emily Prager, Bob Somerby, Joe Walsh

Well, it's too bad the movie studio that made *The Program* hadn't also shot the footage of the Reginald Denny beating, because they could have solved their problem the same way—by just cutting out the highway scene. Of course, things in Los Angeles are never that simple these days. When the trial of the cops who beat Rodney King went against the wishes of the black community, the neighborhoods of South Central erupted. But this week, when the verdicts were lenient toward the black men who beat Reginald Denny, not one rich white person in Beverly Hills started to riot and no black truck drivers were pulled out of their cabs at the intersection of Rodeo Drive and Wilshire Boulevard and beaten with Gucci handbags. The question is, is there a double standard in cases with racial overtones and can juries be trusted anymore to deliver verdicts without intimidation?

• • •

"After the Rodney King jury saw that videotape and the Reginald Denny jury saw their videotape, it's no wonder the National Football League gave up on that instant replay rule."

—Bill

Genetics Defense

First aired 5 · 2 0 · 9 4

**Joe Queenan, Margaret Carlson,
Colonel David Hackworth, Rich Tafel**

With all the sexy scandals in the news lately, the victim defense has put a chokehold on society. TV tabloids are now showcases for victims of abuse, drugs, or fame, kind of like *The Jackson Family Honors.* But now genetic science has handed defendants the most airtight excuse of all—themselves. No longer will anyone need to reveal an abusive husband, a money-hungry boy, parents who drove them to murder by callously eating ice cream in front of the TV. Why? Because the last name in blame is now upon us: genetics. Every day, scientists discover a new gene for something else. There's a gene for homosexuality, a gene for being a thief, even a gene for calling out the wrong name in bed. My question is, if there's a gene for Eric and Lyle Menendez, will we ever manage to convict anyone of anything?

No Televised Trials

First aired 4·22·94

**Charles Peters, Maureen Reagan,
Michael Moriarty, Peter Fonda**

This past week, the Menendez brothers had their faces all over the TV, which is somehow fitting, since that's pretty much how their parents ended up. Of course, most Americans already knew Wally and Beav Menendez, thanks to Court TV, the cable channel for people who think *L.A. Law* is too fast-paced. The problem is, when a trial takes place on TV, the defendant gets judged in the court of public opinion, which means that William Kennedy Smith—who was exonerated—will always be remembered as a panty-shredding drunk. That may score him points with his Uncle Ted, but it's not how the system is supposed to work. Justice is blind, but the camera isn't, and televising trials brands defendants guilty from the start and invariably loses an individual's case to a national cause. Does anyone have a problem with that?

• • •

"The Menendez boys and the state of California have now agreed to let the retrial be decided by Judge Wapner. Judge Wapner isn't used to focusing on the really big crimes, and he's calling this one 'The Case of the Ruined Carpet.'"
 —Bill

Conceding the War on Crime (Needles and Condoms)

First aired 10·6·95

**Janeane Garofalo, Al Franken,
Patti Davis, Bernadette Castro**

Recently there's been a trend in America that I find very disturbing, and I'm not talking about George Bush's kids running for office. No, I'm talking about the trend toward rewarding immoral and illegal behavior when that behavior is simply not as absolutely awful as it could be. For example, we now give free needles to junkies, which seems to me to be only a step away from giving condoms to rapists. In fact, a recent *New York Times* article reported a large increase in the number of rapists wearing condoms, and even a small increase in the number who were calling the next day. My question is, isn't it time we stopped congratulating people for stopping a little short of committing the most heinous crime possible?

Impeach Clarence Thomas

First aired 11·18·94

George Wallace, Lois Romano, Anna Maria Horsford, Lynn Snowden

In his first eighteen months on the Supreme Court, Clarence Thomas spoke up only once during oral arguments—and that was to give a review of *Jurassic Pork*. Thomas may yet prove himself a worthy jurist, but recently a more troubling side of the man has come to light. *Strange Justice,* the new book about Thomas's confirmation hearing, contains so many lurid revelations that many have compared it with the pope's book. According to the authors, Thomas is a lifelong porn freak known for harassing women. And while the judge may still be a role model to some—like conservative Republican senators and James Caan—it now appears he lied under oath. Clarence Thomas is a perv, which I admire—but he's also a perjurer, a harasser, hugely underqualified for the job, and openly bitter in it. My question: Isn't it time we reversed George Bush's biggest boner and impeached Justice Thomas?

• • •

"All men lie, we know that. They can't help it."
—Anna Maria Horsford

Jeffrey Dahmer's Eulogy

First aired 11·29·94

Thank you all for coming. I'll be very brief, because Jeff was never a big talker.

As you all know by now, Jeffrey Dahmer passed away, ironically, after a big Thanksgiving weekend. Some would call him cannibal. Some would call him sodomite. Some would call him sadomasochist or serial killer. And, yes, there was that side to him, but . . . I was his best friend—of the ones who lived—and I think I knew a Jeff Dahmer that the world didn't see. Jeff Dahmer took a big bite out of life. I saw a Jeff Dahmer who was a good friend—if you were down, he'd always lend you an ear . . . or a liver, whatever you needed. I knew the Jeff Dahmer who never took money for the drugs he gave to helpless foreign boys. These are the things you *don't* see.

And no, Jeff was not perfect. He raped and ate people, but it's easy to judge, and maybe someday Jeff will be seen as someone who was ahead of his time, someone who, when it came to the food chain, cut out the middle man. So he ate a little differently than you and I, but, heck, I've got one brother who's a health nut and another who pounds down cheeseburgers—is it that much different? At least with Jeff you could be honest with him. I remember once when I was at a dinner party at Jeff's house, I leaned over and whispered to him, "Jeff, I'm sorry, I just don't like your friends." And he said, "Then just eat the noodles." Sure, Jeff could be biting—or he could have finished lunch.

The point is, it's a dog-eat-dog world out there, and Jeff

was just trying the best he could. And if David Crosby still needs a liver, I think it would be poetic justice if he got it from Jeff. Good-bye, buddy. I hope there's good eatin' in heaven.

A MODEST PROPOSAL

Want a Gun? Get a Musket!

First aired 5·6·94

Well, President Clinton has scored another victory for gun control, and naturally, gun defenders are up in arms about this. And when I say "arms," I'm not kidding. America is a fearful and fearing country because we've let our citizens possess the guns that the military calls firepower: high-powered machine guns of the type only an army has legitimate use for, which, in a perverse way, actually makes sense, because the Second Amendment was written because we had no standing army in 1787 and needed every man to have a gun. But those guns were to be used on the British, not on each other, just in case the British invaded again, which they did in the War of 1812, as you all remember.

What's relevant today is that we now have a standing militia. It's called the National Guard, and even Dan Quayle could beat back today's British, who are not much of a threat anymore, except of course for Fergie. We also have a real army, navy, air force, marines, and thirty thousand nuclear weapons, and if an invader gets by all that, I don't think a guy named Walter with a shotgun is gonna make much of a difference. And yet every single argument against gun control rests on that one line from the Second Amendment that was written for an agrarian nation of five million living by candlelight in homes thatched by mud.

Therefore, I say that if you really insist on keeping this amendment in the Constitution, then we must keep to the

spirit of it, which means you can still own a gun, but it must be a musket. That's what the framers had in mind, so let's see how tough today's gangs are when they have to deal with a weapon that takes some skill to operate. Muskets need to be cleaned every time you use them and then loaded with shot and a musket ball and packed with gunpowder—there's your five-day waiting period.

More to the point, muskets are so unwieldy that if you want to kill someone, you gotta *really* want to kill them. No more reflex shootings over sneakers, no more drive-bys, and one shot to a customer. If we'd had this law in 1963, Kennedy would be alive today and telling a funny story about how he soiled his pants one day in Dallas.

Look, I'm not against the NRA in principle—having tools for killing things around the house is a terrific idea—I'm just saying that today's weapons are so easy to use, it's like hitting from the ladies' tee. Killing is good, of course, but let's save it for the people who are willing to pack their balls in powder to do it.

No, *we* **Can't**

all just

Get

Along

Is Nontraditional English Okay?

First aired 11·19·93

**Joy Behar, Fab 5 Freddy,
Gay Talese, Paul Rudnick**

Language is currently a battlefield in America with implications far beyond how we speak. Back in the days of *Amos 'n' Andy*, Amos could say, "I not only resent the allegation, I resent the alligator," and no one was disturbed by that. But today, alternate language is a serious political issue. Many African-Americans believe that a black kid's "we be" should be considered as legitimate a form of communication as traditional English. On the other hand, cunning linguists like William Safire argue that any diminution of the King's English will only leave its practitioners marginalized from the American mainstream and locked out economically. My question: Who's right?

Campus Self-Segregation

First aired 6·10·94

**Lisa Jones, Roger Corman,
Dave Chappelle, Bob Costas**

In the forty years since the landmark *Brown* v. *Board* ruling, America has made great strides toward ending school segregation, so that today black and white students can sit side by side and cheat off each other's papers. But now minority students at many colleges are asking to live apart in separate dorms, and this disturbing trend threatens to racially divide our campuses like nothing since the last Vanilla Ice record. Martin Luther King had a dream—no, not the one about Eartha Kitt in a catsuit—the other one, the one that said ebony and ivory should live together in perfect harmony, side by side on the piano keyboard or in a college dorm, oh Lord, why can't we? Civil rights pioneers fought and died for desegregation, and to let separatist blacks achieve what George Wallace wanted thirty years ago is just as profound a subversion of our American dream. Does anybody have a problem with that?

• • •

"If blacks and whites can't live together in college, how can they hope to ever live together sober?"

—Bill

Black Leadership

First aired 4·29·94

**Martin Mull, Frank Gannon,
Ruth Shalit, Ken Hamblin**

Nation of Islam spokesman Khalid Muhammad was back in the news after he appeared at the U.S. Holocaust Museum and made a speech so vile, hateful, and offensive that many people thought Ted Danson was working again. We've all heard this kind of inflammatory rhetoric before, but when it comes from a Caucasian like Pat Buchanan, David Duke, or, even worse, Patty Duke, condemnation is usually swift from other white politicians. But, on Mr. Muhammad's "Summer of Hate" tour, when he called Jews "bloodsuckers" and said Hitler was "wickedly great," Louis Farrakhan refused to criticize the content of the speech, Jesse Jackson was slow with a rebuke, and Don King said it made his hair stand on end. The point is, when black leaders fail to criticize virulent hate-mongering, the cause they wind up hurting the most is their own. Does anyone have a problem with that?

· · ·

"Khalid Muhammad's speech got him in some hot water with Louis Farrakhan, because it is strictly against the Islamic code to hate white after Labor Day."
> —Bill

· · ·

"If there is a group of people, Americans, who can least afford to dabble in the arts of racism, it is people who look like me. Black racism is here, it has been tolerated; it's the backlash, the other side of runaway liberalism, and you reap what you sow."
—Ken Hamblin

Malice Toward None

First aired 12·6·94

**Victoria Williams, Eartha Kitt,
Mark Leyner, Terry Anderson**

Two years ago in San Francisco a guy named Doug Hart-
man, an air traffic controller, was in a training workshop,
and he got groped by a bunch of women. It was called the
reverse Tailhook, and Doug was plenty pissed, and he sued
the FAA. Now, I have no idea what this moron is com-
plaining about, but, hey, it's a political world, and every-
body nowadays seems to have an agenda, especially women
and minorities who have a history of being treated badly.
The question is, do they now have the right to even the
score? It's hard to turn the other cheek when you've been
slapped in the face or grabbed in the ass, but in the past,
leaders of oppressed people at least preached the high
road—the high road of, as Lincoln said, "malice toward
none"—and when leaders take that road, like Lincoln and
Martin Luther King and Jesus and Gandhi, we deify them.
Of course, we kill them first, but that's another story. I say
no more getting even; but that's easy for me, I'm a white
guy.

Freedom Fighters or Terrorists?

First aired 10·4·93

Andrea Martin, William Kunstler, Roger Stone, Bob Guccione, Jr.

During the 1992 Democratic Convention, Jesse Jackson stirred his audience with the assertion that one reason so many of the underclass did not fear jail was that to them, jail was not necessarily a step down. In jail, there was less chance of getting shot, a roof over your head, and food three times a day. In other words, jail is not so bad compared with life on the outside, although I'm sure that's not the way Leona Helmsley looks at it. The point is, many of those in the underclass who live in rich, white America see themselves the way Palestinians do in Israel: an oppressed minority under the heel of an occupying army. In Jerusalem, that army is made up of the Israeli defense forces; in South Central L.A., it's the police. Is there a difference?

• • •

"After all these years investigators have just discovered that the truck bomb that destroyed the marine barracks in Lebanon was actually just some NBC guys in a GM pickup."
—Bill

Interracial Adoption

First aired 6·3·94

**Larry Miller, Lisa Sliwa,
Chris Buckley, Sister Souljah**

Interracial adoption sparks controversy because it crystalizes the question of cultural heritage, and, more important, because of what happened to those kids from *Diff'rent Strokes*. Many in the African-American community think that white parents shouldn't adopt black kids because they feel that black children will grow up without a sense of their culture and heritage, not to mention an unnatural fondness for the musical stylings of Yanni. But in truth, isn't it wrong to deny an orphan a loving family for any reason, and shouldn't integration, like charity, begin at home?

• • •

"If you adopt a child, what happens when the marriage goes sour? When Burt Reynolds and Loni Anderson fought, they could always leave Quinton with Dom DeLuise, but what about kids who aren't that lucky?"

—Bill

Code Words

First aired 10·25·94

Paul Rudnick, Rep. Major Owens, LeVar Burton, Cathy Ladman

In the late 1950s and early 1960s, George Wallace, who was then governor of Alabama and not yet that big black comedian, led a crusade for what he called "states' rights." And who could argue with that, except that in the era of civil rights reform, states' rights meant if you were black, the states had rights, and you didn't. "States rights" was a code word for "you Yankees aren't comin' down here and make us go to school with people who we'd still own if you'd kept out of our business in the first place." Fast forward to 1994, and things are better, right? In some ways they are—but now the code words, like saying "urban" when you mean black, masquerade under the guise of political correctness, and around here, that's a capital offense. Don't you agree that using code words is wrong?

• • •

"It depends on whose family. I mean, if you're talking about my family, 'family values' would be a really oppressive thing to live with. It would mean wholesale and lox."

—Cathy Ladman

• • •

"A few years back, GQ magazine was doing a market survey and they became very concerned because it turned out that a lot

of their readership was black and gay. And I remember the code word for it was 'bohemian mix,' which sounded like a pet food in the Village."

—Paul Rudnick

Immigrants

First aired 12·19·93

**Larry Miller, Phyllis Hyman,
Letitia Baldridge, Joe Conason**

America is a nation of immigrants. From every corner of the world the poor, the wretched, and the infirm have clawed their way to our shores. They've become doctors, lawyers, and teachers, except for the most wretched and infirm, who become . . . well, let's leave *Star Search* out of this. But whereas assimilation had always been the goal of immigrants past, today many stay in their insular communities and demand education and services in their native tongues. They seem to want to have their tandoori and eat it too. My question is, if someone comes to the melting pot, is it too much to ask that they melt a little?

· · ·

"There are so many immigrants in New York now, the United States is thinking of opening an embassy here."

· · ·

"The Statue of Liberty, that bitch in the harbor with her arm in the air and what she has written on there . . . People read that thing and they think it's a law. It's not. It's a lovely senti-ment. I read things on public urinals. That doesn't mean I take it to court."

—Bill

A MODEST PROPOSAL

Give the Mexicans New Mexico

First aired 11·12·93

What with NAFTA dominating the news lately, it seems you can't turn on a TV without hearing about an entire class of people who are poorly educated and barely able to speak or write the English language. Of course, I'm talking about the middle-class white people who've been here for centuries.

As for the Mexicans, whenever the issue is trade, the debate always has to dance around the fact that, as Al Gore said the other night, "the American worker is five times more productive than his Mexican counterpart." This disparity in productivity is attributed to better American education, better equipment, and, of course, the ready availability in the United States of illegal Mexican drugs.

But let's face it, all that is just being polite. The real reason Americans are five times more productive is that they work three times as hard. Honestly, when you think of Mexican labor, the phrase "worker ants" doesn't leap to mind. But I'm here to say that the problem is not with the work habits of Mexicans but with the kind of thinking that posits any kind of work as the greatest virtue on the planet. Someone once defined work as whatever you'd rather not do, so who's out to lunch on this one? Well, the Mexicans are, and usually for three or four hours, but that's simply because they come from a different culture, one that lends nobility to the art of napping instead of scorn.

The Protestant work ethic in America has brought us early death rates, stress-induced violence, high blood pressure, type A personalities, three-martini lunches, and the glorification of the "Maalox moment." Ross Perot says he wants the Mexicans to come up to our standards, but is that really a step up? One goal of NAFTA is to stop illegal immigration, but we forget that one reason Mexicans may feel justified in entering our country is that they used to own a big chunk of it before we stole it, fair and square.

Even if NAFTA passes, millions of Mexicans are still going to cross the border, and there's nothing we can do about it, so why don't we just give them New Mexico? It's already got "Mexico" in the title, so who can really blame them for claiming it anyway? It's not new to them, and it looks a lot like Mexico, and it wouldn't take that much effort to cross out the "New" on all the government stationery.

Next thing you know, those industrial standards that Ross Perot is always crying about would even out, and for a change, Americans could start chasing the Mexican dream. Businessmen from Arizona could sneak across the border, and the Mexican Pat Buchanan could whip his people into a frenzy about it, and finally the dream of NAFTA would be realized: an entire continent united behind one cause— those damned Japanese!

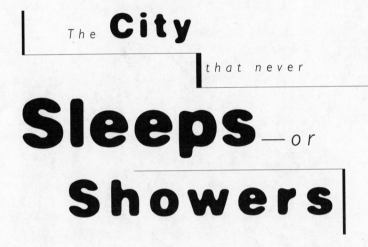

The **City** *that never* **Sleeps**—*or* **Showers**

Cities Obsolete

First aired 7·25·93

**Larry Miller, Robin Quivers,
Jerry Seinfeld, Ed Rollins**

In Franz Kafka's *Metamorphosis,* a man awakes one day to find that he's suddenly turned into a cockroach. Everywhere in the world this is a fantasy, but here in New York, it's a documentary. It is generally agreed in scientific circles that cockroaches, as surely as Sherman took Atlanta, will one day inherit the cities as their own, and now many people are saying, why put off that day? Maybe Gerald Ford was prophetic when he told New York to "drop dead" because, now that we have fax machines, computer networks, picture phones, teleconferencing, and overnight mail, the question has become, why do we need cities at all?

• • •

"Are cities obsolete—no, no, Bill. Because the country will always be boring. Because cows are boring, because grass is boring and farming is dull, Bill, it's dreadfully dull. It will always be dull. No matter how many fax machines you have at the barn, you gotta go out."

—Jerry Seinfeld

• • •

"We should combine cop and garbageman into one job. Because you often see cops walking down the street, they don't have anything to do—grab a broom, start sweeping."

<div align="right">

—Jerry

</div>

The first Politically Incorrect ever, July 25, 1993.

Make Mass Transit a Ride

First aired 10·15·93

In a nation perilously dependent on foreign oil and choking on its own soot, government is always trying to get the American people to take public transportation. But there's one problem with that: We don't like it. If you can get a car, who wants to take a bus? And who can't get some kind of car? Maybe if the bus didn't smell like Yogi Berra's jockstrap, or the subway was a place you could look someone in the eye without worrying that he'd follow you for the rest of your life, people would consider those options. But let's be realistic—we'll be taking speedboats to work before anything like that happens.

And maybe that's the answer right there. If you really want to get the people to take mass transit—make it a ride. Everyone loves going on a ride. It's a ride; of course it's fun. And the only difference between a ride like the Cyclone and the L train in Queens is a couple of loops. What could that cost the city? Whatever it is, it would be made back in days because Americans love to ride upside down and scream and almost vomit when they're on a track. And most of the track is already in place. Put in a few hairpin turns and a blood-curdling descent and people who haven't been to work in years will be standing in line just like they do at Disney World. What is the secret of Disney's parks except a bunch of track and a big rat walking around? And if that doesn't describe the New York City subway, I don't know what does.

Or, even better, flood the subway and put in the Pirates of the Caribbean; there's plenty of pirates down there anyway, it would just be a matter of getting them into the right costume.

Funny, isn't it, how sometimes we work on a problem for years and years and the simple, easy answer is staring us in the face all along.

SOMEBODY'S GOTTA SAY IT

Walls, Malls, and Domes

First aired 8·1·93

I'd like to say a few words tonight about the Biosphere 2. I really don't want to say anything about it because it's so incredibly stupid, but it happens to serve as the best metaphor for an important trend that's going on in this country, and the trend is crawling into some hermetically sealed pod and shutting out the ugliness in America instead of confronting it.

Not to pile on that unfortunate Republican convention last year, but the Astrodome and all such stadium bubbles out in the suburbs are just a poor man's biosphere, and in fact the Astrodome in 1992 was the perfect place for the dish-fest about all the intractable problems that Pat Buchanan said he could eradicate with stern measures alone. Pat, I understand your frustrations. We all hate crime and drugs and people not just like us, but not every form of grime comes up with a steel brush—some things you have to soak overnight.

And while that's going on, it doesn't do any good to hide in domed stadiums or behind the ramparts of "walled communities." Simi Valley is a walled community—it has a wall around it, and I'm sure if the state of California would allow it, they'd build a moat. Again, I understand the impulse.

In America nowadays, one is constantly assaulted for compassion from people begging on the streets, from every damn cause knocking on your door during dinner hour, and

from Hare Krishnas badgering you at the airport. That's why we go to the mall. It's the one safe place where the holy sacrament of shopping shalt not be interrupted. There's no politics in the mall, no flyers, no poster children, no homeless, no hucksters. It is our sanctuary, kind of like the bathroom when you were thirteen. But we should keep in mind that the Romans also built many walls and domes, and even Caesar's Palace now has a mall.

But walls don't keep out problems, they just prolong them. Simi Valley should know better than anyone, because the riot that erupted after the verdict that was read there did not stay behind its ghetto walls. You may think those at the gates are barbarians, and maybe they are, but you better make friends with them because they're coming over.

Squeegee Guys

First aired 3·25·94

**Jonathan Katz, Heather Richardson,
Dana Gould, Peter McWilliams**

Every New Yorker knows the indignity of waiting at a red light, trying to avoid some guy with a sponge and a bucket, and then getting squeegeed against your will. Of course, it's not quite so bad if you're in a car, but it still rubs me the wrong way. Well, now New York's mayor, Rudolph Giuliani, is making himself the Dirty Harry of the squeegee guys. Giuliani's tough—he's saying to the criminals of New York, "Hey, I may not be able to stop all the guns on the street, or any of the murders in the schoolyard, or even stop that kid from stealing the newspaper off my doorstep in the morning, but I'm gonna stand up to *someone*—and it's *you,* squeegee men." Giuliani's opponents say he's taking away livelihoods and sending people into a painful, downward spiral—kind of like what Simon did to Garfunkel—but a civilization is a civilization because it is *civil*! Every little tear in the fabric of society pulls at a thread from the center until our rich tapestry looks like a doormat. Does anyone have a problem with that?

• • •

"Mayor Giuliani's crime-fighting plan is to get rid of all the squeegee guys so that everyone's car looks so crappy no one will want to steal it."

—Bill

New York Sucks

First aired 5·20·94

**Joe Queenan, Jonathan Katz,
Janeane Garofalo, Jeffrey Lyons**

During one nasty week in this brutish winter of 1994, earthquakes in Los Angeles and freezing cold and snow in New York paralyzed both coasts and once again set people to the familiar debate about which city is the most livable. Naturally, New Yorkers sneered at the notion that persistent, obnoxious, predictable, year-in and year-out cold and slush and ice and crap could be worse than one thirty-second earthquake every twenty years, but that's because New Yorkers like being miserable, so bad weather gives them a good excuse. New Yorkers take pride in living in the city that never sleeps—unfortunately, it's also the city that never showers, brushes its teeth, or has good aim when it pees. New York may have been the greatest city in the world in 1958, but it's time somebody noted what an anachronism that claim is today. As a famous New Yorker once said, "New York isn't a Mecca—it just smells like it." Does anybody have a problem with that?

• • •

"Not only was this last blizzard an inconvenience, but the Reverend Al Sharpton charged that the snow was ninety-eight percent white."

—Bill

L.A.'s Decline Is Worse for the Rest of the Country

First aired 3·17·94

**Harry Shearer, John Malkovich,
Suzanne Vega, Ray Bradbury**

Well, Californians have weathered one hardship after another lately—earthquakes, riots, fires, sweeps month—and no doubt many of them must be asking themselves, "With such a hot climate, why all the black leather?" Now, to those who never lived here, California always served this country as our fantasy—like the fantasy of the perfect, beautiful blonde—but then Billy Joel walked in the room. These days, Americans think of Southern California as a dangerous, congested, star-crossed megalopolis, a kind of Cleveland on the Pacific. Like any good fantasy, California has always represented the possible, and so, ultimately, its decline and fall is far more painful to those who dream it than those who live it.

• • •

"I'm really all for analysis . . . I think that kind of knowledge is very, very good. I just think it's used to avoid responsibility for almost anything."

—John Malkovich

L.A. and New York Are Not Leaders

First aired 4·1·94

Martin Short, William Kunstler, Lisa Birnbach, Kurt Andersen

Residents of New York and Los Angeles have long considered themselves America's fashion dictators, which is funny, because even Hitler didn't wear black *all* the time. Whether it's food, clothes, or entertainment, New York and L.A. always think they're light-years ahead of the rest of the country, even though the only trends they've started lately are urban decay and drive-by shootings. After the grunge look became big in Seattle, the tastemakers in New York and L.A. got rich selling pre-ripped jeans to a country too busy to wear out its own clothes. But I say that these two cities aren't really trendsetters, they're fashion surveillance cameras that scout the country for what's hip and then sell it back to the rest of us, always worse for the wear. Does anybody have a problem with that?

• • •

"Fads and trends change so quickly these days. In twenty years, will kids be asking for a big helping of Mom's good old-fashioned Snapple pie?"

—Bill

Pop Quiz Police

First aired 3·15·94

Arianna Huffington, Tim Allen, Ed Asner, Tom Hayden

These days both liberals and conservatives agree that crime could be reduced if there were more cops on the streets to put more criminals in jail. The only difference is that the liberals think the jails should have cable. And on those special occasions when we actually increase police presence—during the Olympics, after jury verdicts, or when the Bulls close in on a championship—crime drops precipitously. Now, we can't afford such a show of force all the time, but couldn't we swing for it every once in a while? Like the pop quiz that always caught you off guard in school, wouldn't the productive fear put into us every once in a while beat the continual fear that we all live in now?

• • •

"The police are strange in Los Angeles. I got pulled over by a cop and he let me off with a warning. He said, 'I should give you a ticket, but you're lucky, I have to get to an audition.'"

• • •

"L.A. is the only town where the cops pull you over and read you your syndication rights."

—Bill

Eating Apple Pie

and the

Girl

next Door

America in Decline

First aired 10·4·93

**Penn Jillette, Michael Elliot,
Fran Lebowitz, Henry Rollins**

In recent years, the marketing people who run the United States government fired the agency that gave us the Vietnam campaign and hired one that, every so often, gives us a virtual Rome of the modern world, vanquishing foes with ease in such hostile climes as Grenada and Panama and Kuwait. In the Gulf War, it didn't really matter that the Iraqi army was surrendering to a *CBS News* crew; the bottom line was, we got one in the "Win" column. Same with the Dream Team—a virtual Olympic Gulf War where we sent an overwhelming force to crush pathetic opponents and then gloat about it. Our insecurity is showing—and given the fact that this country can't educate its children, employ its adults, or make anything that anyone wants to buy, besides weapons, isn't that insecurity well placed, because we are, in fact, already in our era of decline?

• • •

"I'm English, I'm an expert on decline. The royal family would make most of the guests on Donahue and Oprah look good."
 —Michael Elliot

The Pioneer Spirit

First aired 12·18·93

**Jill Brooke, Pat Cooper,
Michael Medved, Michael Lewis**

Last year, 1992, was the cenquicent . . . the sinquent . . . it was the five-hundredth anniversary of Columbus's discovery of the very land in which we now live. And it is a telling comment on our psychological state that the man who for so long had been lauded as a hero for his daring and vision had become, in the language of the land for which he sailed, El Schmuck. Whatever happened to the pioneer spirit in this country? If the pioneers were setting out across America today, they'd need a twelve-step program to cross the Rockies. And Columbus probably wouldn't even get out of the dock because his friends would be telling him, "Chris, you're trying to find new worlds, and you don't know the world *inside* you yet. How about a voyage of self-discovery? Look, there's a group we have, Explorers Anonymous; learn to say, 'I like me,' because the people who only like you because you get them spices aren't your friends anyway." The question is, is the American pioneer spirit gone? And, if so, can we get it back?

Culture of Entitlement

First aired 10·24·93

**Rep. Susan Molinari, Jim Glassman,
Rob Nelson, Dr. Dre**

There's a new craze sweeping America. All the kids are doing it—it's called the Culture of Entitlement. We deserve everything. Farmers depend on subsidies, industries on bailouts, minorities on affirmative action, and wrestlers on steroids. Okay, not all wrestlers. But definitely the bad guys. Haven't Americans come to think of their government as Aladdin's genie in a lamp, capable of granting any wish no matter how absurd?

Manners

First aired 9·19·93

Roseanne, Matt Lauer, Lorraine Bracco, John O'Sullivan

The point of a necktie is that it has no point. It's just there to say "respect," to say, "I want this job," or perhaps, "I want to get in your pants." Restaurants used to make men wear neckties, and it was their way of saying, "We're serious about you getting laid even if you're not. If you want to go home with just a peck on the cheek, go eat at Sizzler." I'm sure women are thinking, Now, if there were only a restaurant that made men not fall asleep ten seconds after sex. Which is just another form of rudeness that has become as common and acceptable nowadays as a tattoo on your ass. My question is, is the downfall in manners merely annoying, or is it a harbinger of the fall of our civilization?

• • •

"Well, I think you're confusing manners with civility, neither of which I like."

—Roseanne

Were the Fifties Our Finest Hour?

First aired 9·5·93

**Adrianne Tolsch, Merrill Markoe,
Andrew "Dice" Clay, Peter Stringfellow**

The 1950s: before the Kennedy assassination, before Vietnam, before Watergate. No wonder Americans pine for this decade—it reminds them of bygone things like employment, literacy, and a time when the only way you could die from sex was by being just a little too good at it. Wasn't Ronald Reagan proof of our longing for a perfect, fifties sitcom Dad? Just like on *Ozzie and Harriet,* he was kindly, fumbling—and you never really knew what he did for a living. But the circumstances of the fifties were a lucky fluke, and they're never coming back, and therefore anyone who plays on the sentimental longing for this era, like Pat Buchanan, is doing his country a disservice. And, therefore, as a traitor, should be shot. Does anyone have a problem with that?

• • •

"The closest these kids come today to civil disobedience is making dinner reservations and not showing up."
 —Bill

The Seventies

First aired 3·16·94

**Dick Clark, Corbin Bernsen,
Quentin Tarantino, Margaret Smith**

Like a dog unearthing a discarded bone, Americans have recently been reliving the 1970s in styles and artifacts. Disco, bell-bottoms, and Tom Snyder are all back, and the question is, why? Sure, some things were better in the seventies; just compare David Koresh with Charles Manson, and you'll see that, at least in the seventies, insane cults made house calls. And the worst thing you could pick up sexually was a little Saturday Night Fever. But when *The Brady Bunch* becomes a Broadway play, surely the end is near. My question is, will Americans get nostalgic for anything, or is there something redeeming about Barry White that we missed the first time?

• • •

"All the styles are coming back. I get nostalgic when I see those bikini underwear ads; they remind me of the Jockeys I wore back in the seventies, when I was just coming into my own."
 —Bill

Why Are We So Miserable?

First aired 11·19·93

**Martin Mull, Joe Conason,
Susan Powter, Dick Cavett**

If the seventies were the "me" decade, then clearly the eighties and nineties have been the "poor me" decades. Every indication of people in pain—drug abuse, alcoholism, insanity, violence, psychotherapy, self-help books—is off the charts. If you're not miserable, then you're in denial. No one knows exactly why we're as miserable as we are, and certainly we can't lay all the blame on Michael Bolton, but the *New York Times* bestseller list now consists of two categories: self-help and Stephen King. My question is, has any nation ever needed so much self-help—and if not, why us?

* * *

"I myself always live every day as if it were my last. Which is why I sleep on a bedpan with a tube up my nose."
—Bill

American Pop Culture

First aired 3·16·94

**Dick Clark, Corbin Bernsen,
Quentin Tarantino, Margaret Smith**

What with the Tonya Hardings and Lorena Bobbitts of the world occupying the news lately, the recent round of GATT trade talks got scant coverage on *Hard Copy*. But here in Shallowville, California, people *were* watching GATT, and this can be attributed to the fact that Hollywood is bilingual; because, after all, money talks, and the French were putting up a big stink about America exporting too much of its culture de crap. Now, you don't have to sell me on how much fun it is to hate the French—after all, this is the country whose actual name used to be Gaul—but have you walked down the street in Paris lately? Me neither, but I hear there's so much American stuff all around—McDonald's, and *Cliffhanger* playing at the movie theater, and Gap ads—that it's enough to make you think you might as well have stayed home. My question is, isn't the greedy exporting of our culture overseas ruining one of the great joys of the world, cultural diversity?

· · ·

"American companies have to modify their products when they sell them overseas for the foreign market. MCI, for example—their ad campaign in France now says, 'Turn in your friends and family.'"

—Bill

• • •

"What I liked about it was the fact that, like, you know, not that it reminded me of home, all right. I tend to think stuff like that is pretty anyway. It's my culture, all right. But then, it also makes it a world culture, all right. We all know, we all know what a Big Mac is, we all know what a Quarter Pounder is, although in France it's called a Royalle with Cheese because they have the metric system, you know."

—Quentin Tarantino

Is the Pope Pop?

First aired 11·3·94

**Neil Peart, Franklin Ajaye,
Elizabeth Wurtzel, Alan Zweibel**

Take a look at any bestseller list these days and you'll find both the Nicole Simpson biography and the pope's new book—each of which dwells quite a bit on sex and, surprisingly, shopping for hats in Brentwood. But these two successes, side by side, may simply mean that even the pope has become pop culture—which may also explain why he often quotes from the *Rick* James version of the Bible. The point is, when the bestseller list is always topped by a comedian or Howard Stern, when *The New Yorker* puts out a fashion issue, when supposedly respected network journalists pursue any lurid angle in the O. J. Simpson case on prime-time news shows, it means that the people we used to look up to are now pandering down to us. In short, pop culture is now the only culture we have.

SOMEBODY'S GOTTA SAY IT

Class

First aired 12·8·93

In Martin Scorsese's film *The King of Comedy,* the central character, Rupert Pupkin, possesses one of the unique tragic flaws in all of drama. Rupert Pupkin, you see, is a man who cannot be embarrassed. He lacks the gene for turning red when he does something stupid, senseless, or classless—and in this, he has apparently become a role model for a nation. How else do you explain seven women, well past the age when they should even be wearing short skirts, sitting on the *Sally Jessy Raphaël* show in string bikinis in order to relate how good they feel about themselves physically? I don't know why they do; I've seen better bodies falling from the *Hindenburg.*

But, of course, it's not their bodies but rather what people reveal about what's in their minds on afternoon television that really makes you shudder for the future of civilization. No perversity or failure, from battered husbands to transvestite bowling teams, is any longer too private a matter to keep to one's self or one's family. More and more Americans find it desirable for a huge audience to bear witness to whatever gooned-out, shallow, pathetic, sick, empty life they're currently leading. Not that we all haven't been gooned-out, shallow, pathetic, sick, and empty at times, but when I was —well, I was embarrassed about it. I tried to hide it. Am I crazy? Maybe some people are just brought up funny.

I know there are those listening to this and thinking that the peccadilloes that bring on embarrassment are not serious offenses, like murder or grand larceny. That may be true, but it is also true that there is a road that leads from offense in the minor transactions of life to even greater moral crimes. The survival of the tribe depends on a kind of private, personal shame that was obviously absent in the mind of the woman in Idaho who abandoned her eighty-two-year-old father with Alzheimer's disease at the dog track, or the yuppie couple who traded their newborn baby for a red sports car, or the "home alone" parents who saw fit to lock their two children in the house over Christmas while they vacationed in Mexico.

It is for people like these—who do not see themselves as criminals—that a sense of embarrassment would have proved helpful, because trading your baby for a car, most of us know, is not just wrong—it's gauche. What would people think? That's what embarrassment *is,* a fear of being mortified by what people will think, and there's nothing wrong with that despite all the nonsense modern psychiatry feeds us to the contrary.

We need guilt and embarrassment and shame to keep us in line. We're not ready for the honor system. Worrying that people might think you're a jerk is not always a bad thing. And sometimes it's the only thing that gets someone to be a mensch.

We ain't

Nothing

but a

Hound
Dog

Dating Young Girls

First aired 12·5·93

**Martin Mull, Joe Queenan,
Henry Rollins, Dr. Joyce Brothers**

Two recent scandals in the news proved the power of love, or at least lust, to be transcendentally potent in the affairs of . . . well, especially of people who have affairs. I mean, what other force on earth, besides sexual attraction, could arise to make soul mates of Woody Allen and Joey Buttafuoco? Joey just doesn't seem like the kind of guy to show up at an Ingmar Bergman festival, but he and Woody could talk about whether a kid should get to have sex before she does her homework. But, as Woody said, "The heart wants what it wants." And my question is, is there any case where the great, unique gift of love should be stifled?

Men Are Pigs, and We're Tired of Apologizing for It

First aired 5·6·94

**Larry Miller, Lisa Sliwa,
Chris Buckley, Sister Souljah**

In the battle of the sexes, it's always open season for women to call men pigs—as if we don't have any feelings. Women say we're sneaky and womanizing and manipulative. I know they do, because I heard a woman say that once when I was pretending to be asleep. If a woman is flighty or moody, they have cute names for that, like "women's intuition" or "feminine mystique." But the fact that we're sex-crazed and horny has no cute name, as if we could help being the way we are any more than a woman can. You want to call us pigs, fine—but I'm tired of apologizing for it. Does anybody have a problem with that?

• • •

"How come, if a woman comes to work in a tailored men's suit, that's considered stylish—but if I show up around here in a simple floor-length gown, I'm weird?"

—Bill

• • •

"I think of pigs as being domesticated, little, kind, wonderful barnyard animals. I think of men as being more like savage beasts."

—Lisa Sliwa

The **O. J.** Simpson **Case:** or, **51** ways to **Leave** your **Lover**

Jock Entitlement

First aired 10·4·94

Bob Costas, Keith Hernandez, Huey Lewis, Gabrielle Reece

Of all the things responsible for O. J. Simpson's demise—the drugs, the women, the late nights with Buddy Ebsen—perhaps nothing is more to blame than America's penchant for treating its jocks like kings. From high school on, athletes learn that cops, coaches, and teachers will always give them a free ride, which probably explains how O.J. got that A in acting class. Professional athletes know they only have to play by the rules *during* the game, and once it's over they can live a lifestyle that would make Rick James blush. I believe it's likely O. J. Simpson committed the crime, because superstar athletes spend a lifetime believing they can get away with anything—and usually they can.

• • •

"If you can play, there's going to be a certain amount of misbehavior that's going to be overlooked. When you get into the pros, you have to commit a felony."

—Bob Costas

GET OVER YOURSELF

Judge Ito

First aired 10·11·94

It's time to give out this week's Prince Rogers Nelson "Get Over Yourself" Award. Our selection tonight is a man who's been thrust into the spotlight as few in the judicial system ever have been before. When Judge Lance Ito was selected as the man who will preside over the trial of the century, it was one of the few decisions in the O. J. Simpson case that wasn't controversial. For once the prosecution and the defense agreed on something: They both liked Judge Ito, and now we know why—because he's as big a ham as they are!

For a man who has the reputation as a no-nonsense judge, Judge Ito's courtroom of late has been filled with nothing but nonsense. For a sitting judge to critique his portrayal on *Saturday Night Live* and say the show hasn't been funny for ten years is preposterous; everybody knows the show hasn't been funny for fifteen years. Furthermore, to allow the defendant to sing show tunes and crack up with his buddies and chat up the jury pool is monumentally inappropriate in a court of law, and just plain rude to the victims.

And when the judge himself offers his view to the defendant that the first juror chosen being number thirty-two was perhaps an omen, it seems to me to cross a very dangerous line between judge and fan, and also to be the height of hypocrisy from a judge who's been railing against the media.

Judge Ito has been threatening to ban the media entirely from his courtroom, but something tells me he'll find a way to save the camera that's on him. And so, for being more a part of the problem than the solution, Judge Ito—get over yourself.

Loyal to a Fault

First aired 11·1·94

**Henry Rollins, Playthell Benjamin,
Elliott Abrams, Mark Curry**

In the last seven days, something amazing happened in American politics: Republicans in the nation's two largest states broke ranks and endorsed Democratic candidates. First Mayor Giuliani in New York came out for Mario Cuomo, then Mayor Riordan in Los Angeles threw his backing to California senator Dianne Feinstein—and this on the heels of Ronald Reagan, John Warner, and other Republicans actively campaigning against Oliver North in Virginia.

To some, this was party treason of the highest order. But to most people I think these actions stand out in this ugly political season as brave and classy—not to mention surprising—among a party that earned a well-deserved bad reputation in the 103rd Congress for putting partisanship ahead of the common good or the truth. It is never easy to break ranks from those with whom you usually stand, but it is often the difference between being great and being a hack; and there is another situation in American life today where breaking ranks would be, to this viewer anyway, a welcome sight.

I'm talking about the O. J. Simpson case, and how, for a guy who never much stood with or for the people of his race, O. J. Simpson has engendered such an amazing solidarity from the African-American community. Most Americans, I think, understand why: Is there a sad and sickening history in America of justice trampled against blacks,

of police brutality, of racism in the highest of places? Yes. There is. Is it understandable that African-Americans would have a deep skepticism about the bringing down of any member of their race, especially one who'd attained so much? Yes. It is.

But that is precisely why it would be so stunning for a black in America today—and I have heard of none so far—to break ranks and put truth and morality above race, and say, despite the sad history of race in this nation, that O. J. Simpson is a singular case, and a case of an indisputably stalking, psychotic wife beater; and, being so, a very likely culprit in murder. It seems that, in the politics of the 1990s, we have all lost sight of the goal of Martin Luther King, who asked that we be judged by the content of our character, not the color of our skin. That's easier for a white to do than a black, I agree, but that set of priorities—character, then color—is what seems to me to have been lost in the O. J. Simpson case.

• • •

"Just being good at football doesn't make you a hero."
—Bill

O.J. Jury Selection

First aired 11·16·94

**Joy Behar, Oliver Stone,
Brent Bozell, Lynn Whitfield**

Well, jury selection was completed last week in the O. J. Simpson case, and some eyebrows were raised when the bench of twelve included only one white guy, prompting a dozing Alan Dershowitz to think that he'd woken up at the Knicks game. Now race, of course, should not matter in matters of jury and justice—but even justice isn't that blind. Race matters plenty, and the question becomes: If it's a fact—as it is—that 70 percent of African-Americans think O. J. Simpson is innocent, then is it any more fair to have him judged by a mostly black jury—including one member who works for Hertz—than it would have been to try John Gotti before a panel of Italian-American plumbing contractors?

· · ·

"For a bunch of people who don't want to talk about it [the O.J. trial], you just can't seem to shut up about it. I really think that's endemic of the whole country—no one wants to talk about it, everyone wants to turn away, but nobody shuts up about it."

—Bill

· · ·

"Let's be honest about it: Ninety-five million people—and I was one of them—watched the stupid white Ford Bronco do forty-five miles an hour for an hour and a half!"

—Brent Bozell

GET OVER YOURSELF

O.J. Law Team

First aired 1·25·95

Well, once again it's time for our Prince Rogers Nelson "Get Over Yourself" Award. Tonight's award goes to a group of men who have done the impossible: embarrassed the legal profession.

When O. J. Simpson's defense team was assembled, people shuddered at the muscle his money could buy: Robert Shapiro, F. Lee Bailey, Alan Dershowitz, Johnnie Cochran, and the rough-hewn bad boy who breaks hearts with a glance—Gerald Uehlman. But when Shapiro started signing autographs outside the courthouse and posing for *Vanity Fair*, it became pretty clear who he thought was the real celebrity in this case. Not to mention laughing it up with O.J. in the courtroom in front of two grieving families. And then Johnnie Cochran got into the act, crying about the Goldmans and the Browns using the media, and then holding interviews with Katie Couric in which *he* was described as the perky one.

But all of this looked positively dignified compared with last week, when Shapiro accused Bailey of horning in on his action, and the two of them called each other names until they had to be separated like kids on a car trip. Can you imagine doctors acting like this—the cardiologist throwing a hissy fit at the neurologist while the patient is choking on his own blood? Man, if I were O.J., I'd wanna *kill* those two.

If there's one true thing O.J. oughta tell these guys, it's not what he did the night of June 12; it's that any good team keeps its problems in the huddle. And, please, if you're gonna keep carping about the media preventing O.J. from getting a fair trial, have the decency to shut the hell up and ignore it. So, to Robert and Lee and Johnnie, remember who this trial is about—the two people who lost their lives and the guy who's paying you to save his—and get over yourselves.

O.J. Jokes

Prosecutors in the O.J. case now say that they will try to prove that O.J. killed Nicole wearing a pair of gloves she bought him for Christmas. Man, what ever happened to just taking something back?

. . .

There are rumors that Robert Shapiro has been demoted on the O. J. Simpson defense team. Shapiro feels he doesn't deserve this kind of treatment and thinks O.J. turned out to be a real backstabber.

. . .

O.J. demoted Shapiro because he was too TV-conscious. O.J. was especially concerned when Shapiro started asking witnesses to answer in the form of a question.

. . .

The name of O.J.'s new book is *I Want to Tell You*. This was chosen over a number of alternatives, including the working title, which was *51 Ways to Leave Your Lover.*

. . .

Judge Ito has ruled that the prosecution can bring up several incidents in which O.J. beat Nicole, and one incident in which O.J. actually beat the Wiz.

• • •

Marcia Clark was furious that, when the jury visited O.J.'s house, a fire was going and fresh-cut flowers were out. She got even madder when Billy Dee Williams showed up with a cold six-pack of Colt 45.

• • •

Ratings for the O.J. trial on CNN have gone up for the third straight week, and all the other networks are scrambling to keep up. In fact, it was just announced that, every day during sweeps week, Regis is gonna bitch-slap Kathie Lee.

• • •

The night of Nicole Simpson's murder, O.J.'s girlfriend Paula Barbieri—who was the Juice's squeeze when he wasn't stalking Nicole—was hanging out in Las Vegas with Michael Bolton. Imagine, if O.J. had known, how close we were to getting rid of Michael Bolton.

• • •

Sixty-one percent of people in Los Angeles think O.J. will walk. The other 39 percent are on his defense team and couldn't comment.

• • •

Lance Ito says he has received a thousand letters begging him to cut off TV coverage of the O.J. trial, and another thousand begging him to make a sequel to *Enter the Dragon*.

• • •

The new book by Faye Resnick is just one of many coming out by people who want to take advantage of their connection to O.J. and Nicole. In fact, you can now get the Al Cowlings Road Atlas.

The Fourth Estate Sale

The *Enquirer* Is Always Right

First aired 11·5·93

Lisa Sliwa, Jonathan Katz,
David Cassidy, R. Emmett Tyrrell

For a publication that everyone claims to despise and disbelieve, the *National Enquirer*'s weekly load of gossip and information still seems to find its way into everyone's consciousness. No one wants to admit that the *Enquirer*'s always right, but if the *Enquirer* says you're dying, don't wait till Monday to get your affairs in order. And speaking of affairs, they never miss one of those either. From Gary Hart to Lady Di to Burt and Loni, the answer to the question "Are the rumors true?" is always the same: The rumors are always true, and the *Enquirer* is always right. Does anybody have a problem with that?

• • •

"Last week the National Enquirer *ran a story that said Hume Cronyn was going to divorce Jessica Tandy because he found out that she was once in a knitting group where they shared needles."*

—Bill

Fame Is the Worst Drug

First aired 3·14·94

**Kelsey Grammer, Cynthia Heimel,
Bruce Herchensohn, Ruth Seymour**

Celebrities and drugs go together in Hollywood like Mom and apple pie do in those backward parts of the country where nobody famous ever ODs. Americans don't hold drug use against their celebrities—Elizabeth Taylor has been in Betty Ford more times than, well . . . Gerald Ford, and she's treated like royalty. But the drugs and the alcohol and the greed and the abusive behavior that fill an entire issue of the *National Enquirer* every week are really just symptoms of the real drug that rules Hollywood—fame. Fame is the most addictive and the most intoxicating drug there is, and although many who are hooked on it claim to disdain it, they seem to do so in a very public manner. It's probably not lost on them that their pleas for privacy just feed the public's desire for the opposite. I say fame is the worst drug of all. Does anybody have a problem with that?

• • •

"Fame has sent a number of celebrities off the deep end, and in the case of Michael Jackson, to the kiddie pool."
—Bill

• • •

"I don't know if I'm addicted to fame; fame is more of an unpleasant circumstance of an addiction to creativity."
 —Kelsey Grammer

"Then why did you go into this business?"
 —Bill

"To save the world."

 —Kelsey

Shake, Rattle, and Die

First aired 10·17·93

**Ben Stein, Mo Gaffney, Jill Brooke,
Christopher Hitchens**

Recently, the heavy-metal band Judas Priest was sued by the mother of a teenage suicide. She claims that it was the lyrics of the hard-rocking band that influenced her son to kill himself. Look, lady, if a kid is that susceptible to the lyrics of a third-rate garage band like Judas Priest, then maybe he needed a little more at-home guidance to begin with. God knows what this kid would have done if he had been listening to a really influential band. When I was in high school, I listened to the Beatles, but I didn't go to class in a walrus suit. Does anyone think there's anything to this nonsense about trying to put responsibility into rock and roll? Irresponsibility is the whole point of rock and roll! Does anyone have a problem with that?

• • •

"These days, the kids are listening to the yeah-yeah-yeah music, the way-out hard rockers like Guns and Ammo and Sister Soultrain."

—Bill

Journalists as Auteurs

First aired 1·28·94

**Al Franken, Sam Donaldson,
Harriet Woods, Bob Dornan**

In the early days of television news, reporters were our eyes and ears. They didn't give us analysis or entertainment, and you never saw Edward R. Murrow talking to someone clad only in lace or lingerie, unless it was J. Edgar Hoover. But somewhere along the line, reporters became more of the story than the story itself, and now when some pompous, self-important ABC newsman like Brit Hume stands in front of the White House, you get the feeling he's not so much there to bring you the news as the news is there to bring you him. If these reporters really took seriously the pride they claim in being journalists, they'd go back to doing what journalists do—reporting the facts for people who can't be on the scene and letting the audience make up it's own mind. Does anyone have a problem with that?

. . .

"We live in a world where the line between news and entertainment has been eaten away like David Crosby's septum."
 —Al Franken

. . .

"News reporters have become more important than the stories they cover. This phenomenon reached acute proportions a couple of years ago when Variety *referred to the Gulf War as 'a Wolf Blitzer vehicle.'"*

—Bill

GET OVER YOURSELF

Howard Stern

First aired 12·16·94

Well, once again it's time for our Prince Rogers Nelson "Get Over Yourself" award. Tonight the award goes to a man who made his name being funny but is now beginning to take himself just a little too seriously. When Howard Stern first became a big deal on the radio, it was because at a time of suffocating neo-puritanism, people all over the country connected with the idea that *no* idea was too sacred. Also, Lesbian Dial-a-Date was pure genius. But adulation has now seduced Howard into believing that he's something much, much more than what he is—a funny disc jockey.

It's bad enough when a comedian can influence elections as Howard did with both Christine Todd Whitman and George Pataki, flexing his ego to demonstrate that he can bring his followers into the voting booth as easily as he can get them to undress in the studio. But *running* for governor, as Howard also did—now we're starting to get into Ross Perot dementia, the love affair one develops with the sound of one's own voice describing over and over again what would get done "when *I'm* king."

Given this history, it's no wonder that Howard's latest foray into lifesaving has caused some alarm that the next move for the king of all media may be a cult on the order of Jim Jones's or David Koresh's. Howard, don't make people drink poisoned Kool-Aid, even if it's on Pay-Per-View—and stop buying into the hype you yourself created. Go back to being the

perverted, lesbian-loving, butt-bongo-playing, scatalogically obsessed, insecure, imagining-everyone's-ripping-you-off, egomaniacal, rock-star-wannabe, horny Jewish guy you always were, because, after all, we don't want you to get over yourself too much.

Cum

as

you

Are

For the first week, I did the monologue with cards in my hand.
Politically incorrect, or just stupid?

Sex Addiction

First aired 8·22·93

**Michael Medved, Lisa Sliwa,
Sean Kelly, Joe Franklin**

The so-called recovery movement is the greatest thing to happen to horny people since the cigarette. Because what used to be regarded as mere "sleaze-baggery" has now been reclassified under the kinder, gentler rubric of "sexual addiction." Such luminaries as Michael Douglas, Wade Boggs, and Steven Tyler of Aerosmith have all pled guilty to this "crime." But, if you ask me, the real crime here is taking the beautiful, natural act of getting absolutely as much tail as you possibly can, and calling it a disease. I guess wanting to watch a beautiful sunset every night is a solar addiction now.

• • •

"You know you're a sex addict when you find yourself standing in Times Square thinking, There's nothing much to do here."
—Bill

Strippers

First aired 9·5·93

**Adrianne Tolsch, Merrill Markoe,
Andrew "Dice" Clay, Peter Stringfellow**

It's safe to say that most women don't give female strippers a lot of points for upholding feminism. And yet feminism is all about women being respected and gaining more control. How, then, would it square this picture? A woman, confident enough to stand naked before a stranger, dances for two minutes and then leaves with twenty dollars of his money, no G-strings attached. Take the same guy who around the office is always grabbing a little heinie by the coffee machine, and put him in a high-class strip club, and he becomes as incapable of initiative as Ted Kennedy in a crisis, sitting there like a mounted elk and drooling into his lap, which also is too intimidated to rise up. As hard as this one is to swallow, the truth is: Out of all women in the workplace, strippers get the most respect on the job.

• • •

"You know the art of exotic dancing is catching on all over the world. In Iran now they're having wet veil contests."
—Bill

Masturbation

First aired 9·12·93

**Curtis Sliwa, Larry Miller,
Jerry Seinfeld, Dr. Wilbert A. Tatum**

Feminists have long argued that pornography objectifies and dehumanizes women and, in so doing, makes violence against them easier to commit. Men, however, know this is a crock. On the contrary, pornography acts as a release valve on the overinflated balloon of male sexual tension by pulling tidal waves of angry life force from millions of men each day that would otherwise be targeted for unwilling receptacles. In other words, every stroke book stops a rape. Anybody got a problem with that?

• • •

"I'll tell you how I feel about porn channels. They don't educate us, they don't enlighten us, and they don't come in clearly enough where I live."

—Bill

• • •

"If it wasn't for masturbation, most men wouldn't know that anything could happen."

—Jerry Seinfeld

NAMBLA

First aired 6·22·94

**Martin Short, William Kunstler,
Lisa Birnbach, Kurt Andersen**

A recent scandal here in New York involved high school teacher Peter Melzer, a thirty-two-year veteran of teaching with an exemplary record, who was fired for being a member of the North American Man Boy Love Association. And this brings to mind two questions: one, how could anyone be a pedophile; and, two, what exactly is the club's secret handshake? Now, certainly Mr. Melzer is no Boy Scout—although I'm sure that's not for lack of trying—but his very public dismissal has caused a tidal wave in the kiddie pool, with him trying to hold on to his job and getting sand-bagged when Liz Taylor leaped to his defense. Society has made it a law that the only people who can act on their love for young boys are young girls, so the question is, if a person doesn't break that law, should he be fired for having beliefs that are just plain creepy?

• • •

"The NAMBLA teacher said he never made a pass at any of his students—although he did once demonstrate how some natural objects increase in size as they get closer to the son."
—Bill

Couch

Potato

Famine

Birth of a Nation |

First aired 10·29·93

Joe Queenan, Michael O'Donoghue, Jim Morris, Lynn Martin

Resolved: The past is past. Whether it's a national embarrassment such as slavery, or a personal embarrassment like that Xerox of your ass you made at last year's office Christmas party, any attempt to airbrush history to suit contemporary tastes always rings false. This week, D. W. Griffith's famous silent movie *Birth of a Nation,* which was made in 1915, was pulled from a Library of Congress festival because of its sympathetic portrayal of the Ku Klux Klan. No one disputes that the Klan is favorably represented in the film—in fact, its original title was *Boys in the Hoods*—but the moods and mores of 1915 were what they were, and repressing the past just gives it more power today. Does anyone have a problem with that?

* * *

"The Birth of a Nation *got pulled from a film festival because of the way it portrays the KKK, and many people are protesting. The film industry in Mississippi said it was a shame, but there were no longer any good roles being written for Klansmen."*
— Bill

Who Killed JFK?

First aired 8·22·93

**Michael Medved, Lisa Sliwa,
Sean Kelly, Joe Franklin**

When it comes to the Kennedy assassination, there are so
many good suspects: the CIA did it, the Mafia did it,
Castro, the Russians, LBJ. There's even one wildly radical
theory now that it was a lone gunman named Oswald. And
then there's Oliver Stone. He believes they all did it, kind of
like the way in *Batman* all the crooks in the city join forces
in an underworld alliance of evildoers. And they have a lair.
To kids today who believe only in celluloid and who con-
sider books "slow TVs," Oliver Stone is the Arnold Toynbee
of his age. Forget pornography, isn't this how movies are
really dangerous?

Westerns

First aired 3·4·94

**Bob Somerby, Lynn Martin,
Letitia Baldridge, Gene Siskel**

After riding tall in the saddle for decades on movie and television screens, the Western all but disappeared in the late 1960s, and for years, if you wanted to see a simple tale about a man and a horse, you had to go to one of those theaters on Forty-second Street. Now the Western is back in vogue, and through pictures like *Last of the Mohicans* and *Unforgiven,* we get to learn new things, such as it was the Iroquois who invented the Salad Shooter. But the question is, why has the Western rolled back into town? In an era of rampant crime, is it our yearning for a simpler time, when you could hear a drive-by shooting coming up the road, or is it just because we love those fabulous Ralph Lauren ads?

Media Violence

First aired 2·18·94

Joe Queenan, Jonathan Katz, Janeane Garofalo, Jeffrey Lynn

The Clinton administration has taken a lot of heat for its get-tough stance on Hollywood violence, but its approach seems to be working. Warner Brothers has just announced that their big summer blockbuster is going to be called *Lethal Weapon 4: Death by Natural Causes*. Some have accused the president of advocating censorship, but I say it's about time that filmmakers got this long-overdue spanking. Hollywood is a self-serving, hedonistic town with no regard for the morals that anchor American society—that's certainly why I live there—but allowing the entertainment industry to dictate our country's values is like taking career advice from Shelley Long. Like the arm-twisting presidents that history admires, Bill Clinton is simply staring down a reckless group into playing by the rules. That's not censorship, that's leadership. Does anyone have a problem with that?

• • •

"Clinton and Reno have really scared people in the television industry. Fox just announced they're changing the name of one of their big shows to Rescue 411. *In the first episode, the Fox cameras capture a couple in the act of frantically calling information for the address of a restaurant when they're late for dinner."*

—Bill

Critic as Auteur

First aired 3·18·94

**Michael Medved, Martin Mull,
Shelley Winters, Jim Vallely**

The media in this country have long had the power to create stars, and don't think Christian Slater isn't thankful. But somewhere in this star-studded universe, we've forgotten who revolves around whom, and so it's become that the real story is no longer the star, it's the critics—what roles *they* like for Drew Barrymore, what *they* had for lunch with her, why *they*'d like to give her a smack in the face. The Book of Revelation says, "When the critic becomes the star, and two-headed beasts with thumbs that go up and down rule the world, the end is near." So, isn't the end near?

• • •

"They asked Louis Farrakhan what he thought of Schindler's List, *and he said it was the feel-good hit of the season."*
—Bill

• • •

"Frankly, I'm embarrassed by my profession."
—Michael Medved

Romance Is More Damaging Than Violence

First aired 3·18·94

Michael Medved, Martin Mull, Shelley Winters, Jim Vallely

Violence as entertainment in television and films has recently inspired an outcry for industry policing, but everyone is missing the big picture here. The real destructive force in movies is not violence, it's romance, or rather the unrealistic depiction of romance—in movie parlance, the Big Thaw. That's what every romantic comedy is built around: From *It Happened One Night* to *The African Queen* to *When Harry Met Sally,* the plot is always the same. Boy meets girl, girl hates his freakin' guts, she despises him, he's dirt beneath her heel—and then they get married. Now, in the movies, it takes an hour and a half for this transformation to take place, and a mismatched couple—say, a drunken ex-marine and a social-climbing South American manicurist—work out their differences. In real life, she cuts off his penis! Fairy tales in movies have caused more romantic damage than Gloria Steinem. Does anybody have a problem with that?

• • •

"In a speech the other day, Janet Reno said she thought that the movies and television were way too violent. Then, out of the blue, she said she also was just getting sick of Winona Ryder."
—Bill

Forrest Gump

First aired 10·5·94

**Lisa Sliwa, Roy Blount, Jr.,
Allen Ginsberg, Marc Maron**

Americans usually have two complaints with the movies they see: They're far too violent, and they don't feature enough nude scenes with Wilford Brimley. But lately, Hollywood has been selling us something really strange and ugly, and I'm not talking about Gerard Depardieu. No, America has fallen in love with Forrest, Forrest Gump, a charming moron whose misguided message is that it's easy to get ahead in life if you're a brain-dead simpleton, and that's bad advice, even if it did work for Ronald Reagan. The point is, at this especially stupid juncture in our nation's history, with SAT scores down and *Baywatch* ratings up, the last thing America needs is to glorify dumbness. Does anyone have a problem with that?

• • •

"People are flocking to this movie because Forrest Gump reminds them of every man they know. No one is saying this is a bad example of American manhood."
—Lisa Sliwa

TV vs. Movies

First aired 3·18·94

**Michael Medved, Martin Mull,
Shelley Winters, Jim Vallely**

With the unexpected success this year of such films as *Schindler's List* and *Philadelphia,* 1994 should be a good year for people who want to make serious movies. But then one of those movies will bomb badly, and in 1995 we'll see Burt Reynolds in his old hair chasing Dom DeLuise in a leotard. For now, the movies can crow that they're the medium that's dealing with the real issues, but the truth is, their bastard stepson, television, is the real breaker of barriers. TV did the movie *An Early Frost* eight years before *Philadelphia,* and the miniseries *Holocaust* fifteen years before *Schindler's List.* Ninety-nine percent of TV is dreck, but the 1 percent that isn't is way ahead of the movies every time. Does anybody have a problem with that?

AIDS Ribbons

First aired 12·19·93

**Larry Miller, Phyllis Hyman,
Letitia Baldrige, Joe Conason**

Gil Cates, the producer of the 1993 Academy Awards tele-
cast, said that Hollywood's Susan Sarandon, Tim Robbins,
Richard Gere, and others who used the broadcast as a polit-
ical forum will not be invited back as presenters. If that's the
case, given Hollywood's lock-step allegiance to wearing
AIDS ribbons at the Oscars, shouldn't they just cancel the
whole event? After all, the last time a political movement
demanded solidarity by making everyone wear a piece of red
cloth, Poland got invaded. My question is, why should
AIDS, as awful as it is, take over our lapels in precedence
over every other issue? And should even the most important
of causes be thrust into our consciousness at moments when
we are, after all, just trying to be gay?

The Real Oscar
Acceptance Speech

First aired 3·18·94

Wow, thanks. I'm so excited. I'm glad I'm loaded. This is great. I have to tell you, two years ago, when my agent came to me with this script—well, if anybody had told me I'd be standing here now, I would've said, "Yeah, right. And Spielberg's Oscar movie would be about a human monster." Also, I would've probably read the script instead of just giving it to my wacky girlfriend on the beach in Nevis.

This is a project that, quite frankly, nobody believed in, and I think I know why. It sucked. But thirteen monkeys with Guild cards sat in a room with typewriters for two years and somehow managed to make me likable. So, let me just quickly mention a few people. My agent at CAA: Jack, you spend more time on your wardrobe than you do on my career. Consider yourself fired. And, yes—that woman in my car was your assistant, and yes, she does hate you.

My director on the picture: Graham, you give malicious, egotistical arrogance a bad name, and everybody I know wishes you nothing but pain. But may I say that professionally, you couldn't direct a column of ants to a melting Hershey bar. I know I'm running long here, and I don't want to cut into Richard Gere's musical tribute to the Dalai Lama—but there's a few more people I want to mention:

The producers, who, as always, only cared about saving their own asses and staring at everyone else's.

The cast: When we were on the set, it was like being with family, which I guess is why we fought all the time and ate dinner in silence.

Our crew: Guys, I can't remember any of your names, and I have no idea what any of you did when you weren't sitting on your asses eating bagels and M&Ms, but the next time you say "we" made this picture, just chuckle to yourself a little bit, okay?

My new bride: I love you very much, but don't wait up tonight, if you know what I'm saying. I earned this one.

My parents: Without you, I wouldn't be here, but that's just science. If I had listened to you, I'd be at a Radio Shack in Teaneck and reading Time/Life books to fix my own toilet!

Finally, to the academy: I think I know why you voted for me—because De Niro didn't play a twitching gimp this year. Also, you knew that you screwed me once before and you heard that I was possibly ill. Well, that was the best story I ever planted. I'm actually fine, thank you, and now I have a damn Oscar. You can find me at the bar.

Nontraditional Casting

First aired 6·24·94

**Tom Rhodes, Floyd Brown,
F. Murray Abraham, Rich Hall**

When Rodgers and Hammerstein wrote *Carousel,* they never thought of it as a revisionist tale of racial harmony. However, the show's current Broadway revival features thirteen black people living happily in nineteenth-century Maine, which is funny, because even today there aren't thirteen black people in Maine. What's going on here is nontraditional casting, a directorial choice that puts minorities in parts usually denied to them. In *Carousel,* this means that one third of the roles are played by actors of color, and if that's not bad enough, there are three straight guys in the men's chorus. Supporters of color-blind casting say it gives minority actors more chances to work, but in reality, it distorts the playwright's vision and subverts historical truth. It's affirmative action with dance numbers and fancy clothes— and that's not progress, that's RuPaul! Does anyone have a problem with that?

• • •

"Who would've expected that Woody Allen, who started on Broadway in Play It Again, Sam, *would now be playing in* Miss Saigon"?

—Bill

GET OVER YOURSELF

Mickey Rourke

First aired 11·10·94

Once again it's time for our Prince Rogers Nelson "Get Over Yourself" Award. Tonight's award goes to a man who absolutely cannot get arrested, but still spends most of his time trying. When Mickey Rourke stopped acting—you know, right after *Diner*—he skipped off to France, where his five-day stubble and silicone-implanted cheeks apparently looked sexy instead of stupid. Then he took up boxing—a sport where the term "class" refers only to your weight, which he proved by beating up his wife, Carré Otis, because, hey, he had to win a bout somewhere. And as if all that weren't tasteless enough, he also made *Wild Orchid.*

Now, the whole thing just seemed like some bad Euro-trash lovers spat that had blown over—until last week, when he took the same act on the road: He stalked Ms. Otis through the New York fashion shows, all the while *claiming* it was all because of his interest in ready-to-wear clothing, made sixteen-year-old models kiss him for the paparazzi, and, finally, threw a $20,000 fit in his Trump Plaza hotel room, all because there was nothing good on Spectravision. Mickey, you're boring us. Get yourself a shower and a shave, and for once—get over yourself.

A MODEST PROPOSAL

Put Death Row Prisoners on Broadway

First aired 12·6·94

These days, everything's so crazy, I'm lucky I can spell "kook" backward. On the one hand, prisons are so overcrowded that in order to get solitary, you've got to cough up first and last months' rent; on the other hand, Broadway theaters are so empty, the producers of *Damn Yankees* have had to institute Bat Day.

Now, I'm not saying which of these problems is more urgent, but it does seem that we can probably kill two birds if we just do what, to me, seems the obvious and most practical thing: put death row prisoners on Broadway. Not in the seats, on stage. As extras. Extras who get killed. Really killed.

Now, to those of you who say we're violating the Eighth Amendment, well, okay, maybe this punishment is a little unusual, but it's hardly more cruel than hanging or getting zapped in an electric chair. That's not unusual? Sit down, take a load off—die. Fatal furniture is definitely unusual. So I say, why not alleviate prison overcrowding and, at the same time, give death penalty–loving Americans what they and what the prisoners really want?

Whether it's the beheading scene in *Les Miz,* or the *Cats* that apparently *don't* have nine lives, every psycho in jail can finally have what he craved to begin with—his fifteen minutes of fame. And just think of all the new productions that

will send people to the theaters in droves, shows like *Death of a Salesman and Several Annoying Customers; The Will Rogers Follies that Lead to Horrible Fatalities; Good-bye, Dolly; Fiddler* Off *the Roof;* Neil Simon's *Broadway Bound and Gagged* and *Body Found Barefoot in the Park.* The list goes on. Perhaps too long. Look, if we want to take a bite out of crime, it's time we let criminals start chewing scenery.

We *Love*
to get
High,
and it
Shows

Freedom to Live Intensely

First aired 3·11·93

Jim Morris, Timothy Leary, Sally Kirkland, Rep. Marjorie Margolies-Mezvinsky

Living a long, healthy life has generally been regarded as a goal by most people, but now in America it's fast becoming a law—or actually a bunch of laws. Smoking laws, seat belt laws, motorcycle helmet laws, laws against drugs—not to mention all the hell Dr. Kevorkian gets. Now, I'm not recommending excessive drinking, illegal drugs, and fast women—although they've always worked for me—but isn't America all about at least having the choice? Right about now, wouldn't you rather be John Belushi than Chevy Chase? And whether you're a boxer who risks brain damage, or a football player who uses steroids, or an artist who uses drugs to enhance his creativity—shouldn't the right to live intensely and die young be as sacred as anything else in the Bill of Rights?

• • •

"I think we all admire the Rolling Stones for keeping at it in their fifties, but their fans are too old to be buying souvenirs. Even if you did, would you really want to get that colostomy bag with the big red tongue on it?"

—Bill

That's Mom's Job

First aired 10·20·94

**Floyd Brown, Linda Doucett,
Mykel Board, Rolonda Watts**

These days, as more and more parents abandon their traditional duties, the government has started wasting time and money providing us with the advice that Mom used to give us: Wear your seat belt, wear a helmet, don't drink, don't drink and drive, don't have sex, don't do drugs, don't smoke, and stop that or you'll go blind! In what started out as a well-intentioned attempt to deal with the breakup of the family, the government is now teaching us what we used to learn at the kitchen table—whether it's sex education, nutritional advice, or why Daddy is living with his secretary. The point is, the government is treating us like children, and that's Mom's job. Does anyone have a problem with that?

Sue Twinkies Too

First aired 11·2·94

Kennedy, Joe Bolster, Playthell Benjamin, Thomas Dolby

Everyone these days seems to be jumping on the nonsmoking bandwagon—in the latest cigarette ads, even the Marlboro Man is wearing the patch. It's common knowledge that cigarettes increase your chances of getting lung cancer, heart disease, and, of course, a date with Shannen Doherty—yet tobacco companies are now being sued for the negative effects of their products. But is smoking the only thing that causes health problems? What about the guy who Twinkies himself to death? What about people who OD on their morning coffee? The fact is, fattening foods, coffee, cigarettes, and alcohol are all abused in this country, and sometimes at the same sitting—but enough about John Madden. I say, if you want to litigate against tobacco companies, fine, but you damn well ought to be able to sue the size 46 pants off the makers of anything else that increases cholesterol, blood pressure, or tooth decay. Does anybody have a problem with that?

• • •

"Remember Desenex had that commercial, 'Athlete's foot? Don't blame Desenex.' Which was kind of snooty. It's like, 'Pregnant? Don't blame Trojan.' I say, if you're using a condom and it's defective and you have a kid, you can sue them. In fact, let them keep the kid!"

—Joe Bolster

Sin Deductions

First aired 6·3·94

**Larry Miller, Lisa Sliwa,
Chris Buckley, Sister Souljah**

Well, by now tax season is just a bad memory—the forms, the filing dates, and the carnage left by jubilant accountants "wilding" in the streets . . . But when it comes to ways of collecting more money, President Clinton's favorite buzzword is still the "sin tax," which would discourage smoking, drinking, and just about anything else that keeps the registers ringing in this country. The sad truth is, virtue doesn't turn a profit, so I say what we really need on the 1040 form is a sin deduction—a simple way of rewarding people for getting stewed, screwed, tattooed, or doing anything where you leave a tip in someone's waistband. The sin deduction: stimulate the economy while we stimulate ourselves—does anybody have a problem with that?

Sin vs. Disease

First aired 10·10·93

**Mark Kostabi, Merrill Markoe,
John Lawton, Marvin Kitman**

America has become a country where everything that used to be a sin is now a disease. The Ten Commandments? Oh, you mean the 120 steps. In a kind of psychological version of the way the government renames certain expenditures so they won't have to be counted in the budget, Americans have found a way to sin "off book." Drunks are now alcoholics, thieves are compulsive borrowers, and Senator Bob Packwood is a sex addict who's recovering from the compulsion to give job interviews to young girls in motel rooms. And, before he died, Jeffrey Dahmer had just enrolled in Overeaters Anonymous. My question is, isn't the reclassification of sin as disease really a shameless attempt to deflect blame for stupidity, remarket vice as virtue, extort compassion from slobbering fools, and, worst of all, sell books?

• • •

"It turns out that all those times Woody Allen talked about masturbating, he was actually having sex with his inner child."
 —Bill

Smoking

First aired 4·1·94

Martin Short, Caleb Carr, Marion Winik, Jimmy Breslin

The war against smoking has now escalated from greatly restricted smoking areas to actual discussion about the prohibition of something 46 million Americans enjoy every day of their own free will—and another 20 million bum them. The trade-off between health and pleasure is a privileged decision that each of us makes in his own way, and to non-smokers who seem to have such callousness toward smokers, let me ask you: How would you feel if you were denied the little pleasures that make your everyday life bearable? What if you suddenly weren't allowed your coffee in the morning, or that crossword puzzle you do on the bus, or touching yourself while watching the Weather Channel? What if it became against the law to watch a certain soap opera every day, or shoot hoops in the driveway, or sit on the washing machine with no pants on? What would your life be like if suddenly you were a criminal for the crime of girl-watching on your lunch hour or administering a champagne enema before a shower? I ask you, hath not a smoker eyes? Hath he not organs, dimensions, senses, passions? If you prick us, do we not cough?

• • •

"This week, they're talking about banning cigarette smoking in any place that's used by ten or more people a week—which I guess means Madonna can't even smoke in bed."

"Senators from tobacco states are always against AIDS research. Apparently, Jesse Helms and Strom Thurmond wish AIDS patients could be happy with lung cancer like everyone else."
—Bill

Writers always have a home on Politically Incorrect.

Smokers' Rights

First aired 10·4·93

Penn Jillette, Michael Elliot, Fran Lebowitz, Henry Rollins

Many people in this country engage in legal activities that annoy bystanders: smoking, drinking, playing loud music, or, down here in the Village, wearing those leather pants with the butt cut out. Recently, a movement has begun to protect onlookers from those activities they find bothersome. Smoking is relegated in most restaurants to a smoking section, as if there weren't equal call for a no-eating-like-a-pig section, or a no-buying-her-dinner-just-to-get-laid section. In addition, beer drinking has been segregated in baseball stadiums, anti-noise ordinances passed for boom boxes, and Congress, as I speak, sits in session on the exposed butt issue.

• • •

"I just quit smoking . . . crack."

—Bill

• • •

"There used to be a lot of things people believed in that had to do with truth, honor, hard work—and now they just believe in not smoking."

—Fran Lebowitz

• • •

"The two things that the middle class is most concerned about are smoking cigarettes and wearing fur coats. These are the burning issues of the middle class."

—Fran

"And smoking fur coats."

—Penn Gillette

• • •

"It's easy to tax cigarettes because it's hard to cheat on your cigarette taxes."

—Fran

• • •

"What about meat? What about people who eat steaks? What about people who drink martinis? What about people who have stress because they don't have enough sex? There's a million ways to kill yourself, and when you come down to it, America causes cancer. It's everything we do, and put in our bodies, and live with."

—Bill

Drunk Is Funny

First aired 11·3·94

**Neil Peart, Franklin Ajaye,
Elizabeth Wurtzel, Alan Zweibel**

Of all the things they don't have today that they had twenty years ago—Ed Sullivan, disaster movies, serious Afros, Ted Kennedy's presidential hopes, the Bee Gees, and real breasts—the thing I miss the most is drunks. We don't have any drunks anymore, just alcoholics. Which is a shame, because drunks were great. Drunks were funny, and that's why so many beloved show business figures in the past became beloved by playing drunk, like W. C. Fields and Foster Brooks and Otis on *Andy Griffith,* and Yeltsin. They brought laughter to millions, but then certain grinches stole that—and people who make the rest of us feel guilty for laughing at things that are funny are nothing more than grinches who steal enjoyment from everyone because they had a problem with something. Well, we all have tragic associations with something—even a chicken can be made to seem tragic if your father was killed choking on an egg. Drunks are funny—I say we bring them back and let Dudley Moore have a career again.

• • •

"William Holden got drunk, hit his head on the coffee table— dead. I mean, does it get any funnier than that?"
 —Bill

A MODEST PROPOSAL

Drunk-Driving Lane

First aired 4·15·94

According to a recent article in *The New York Times,* by the year 2003, guns will pass cars as America's leading killer. Not surprisingly, this piece of news has led to more calls for handgun restrictions and, from drunk drivers, demands for a recount. Now, no one in his right mind would ever defend driving drunk—and I wouldn't, either. But I do think a sense of balance has been lost on this issue.

Of course, the penalties for drunk driving should be strict, but with the allowable level of alcohol in your blood being lowered each year, you no longer need to be exactly drunk to get arrested, and many states are moving toward a zero blood level. Count on it: The politicians will make this happen because it's easy to be righteous about this. What's harder is to be right about it.

Now, does any amount of liquor impair your best driving? Probably. But so do about fifty other things. Would you rather face a guy who had two beers coming at you, or someone rocking in his seat to music that's way too loud? Or perhaps someone driving away from a major domestic breakup, with tears streaming down his face? My God, I see women putting on eyeliner while they're driving; people talk on the phone while they're driving, they eat, they flirt, they have sex in trucks. Are there laws against any of these things? No.

If we all want to be 100 percent alert when we're driving, then we should be consistent about it, especially since drinking and driving is so woven into our way of life: Clubs have two-drink minimums, bars have happy hours, and key chains come with bottle openers. Anheuser-Busch wants you to "Know When to Say When," but drown yourself in icy-cold beer until it's time. So, aren't we just kidding ourselves when we pretend to completely separate drinking from driving?

Instead of trying to get everyone who's had a belt off the road, why not just give us Third Avenue and the shoulder of the FDR Drive? Or whatever the streets are in your area. Give us a couple of streets where there's a drinking lane, sort of like the bunny slopes for bad skiers. In fact, if you just drop the drinking lane down a couple of feet from the rest of the roadway, drunks would end up in there, naturally, like a gutter ball. On the really big interstates, maybe even two or three drinking lanes, "buzzed," "blitzed," and "blind." Safety and fun don't have to be at odds with each other, and if we would just institute these changes, America could get going on a solution to dull parties—something I call the "designated drinker."

Outer Child: In Praise of Oblivion

First aired 3·17·94

**Harry Shearer, John Malkovich,
Suzanne Vega, Ray Bradbury**

George Bernard Shaw once observed that "the secret of being miserable is having the time to wonder about whether or not you are happy," which is probably why he never got his own game show. The point is, our modern obsession with finding the inner child runs counter to nature's own very effective means to tranquility: oblivion. The human mind is a marvelous mechanism that usually serves us well by blocking out the pains of the past, and if you don't believe me, when was the last time Bachman-Turner Overdrive popped into your head? Picking at our mental scabs is largely a yuppie indulgence—like a BMW or a juicer—and if we would just let the inner child sleep, maybe we'd have a little more peace around here for that person who has to face the world—the outer adult.

• • •

"Everyone who gets in trouble nowadays blames it on some childhood trauma or form of abuse. It's gotten to the point where I feel left out—either I've blocked out the memories, or my parents just never found me attractive."

—Bill

Listening to Prozac

First aired 11·12·93

**Arianna Huffington, Dr. Peter Kramer,
Harry Shearer, Jim Traficant**

Over the last few years, Americans have begun exploring alternatives to psychotherapy. Because who wants to spend a lifetime on the psychiatrist's couch, unless you're looking to get picked up? This week, one of the fastest-rising books on *The New York Times* bestseller list is *Listening to Prozac,* a chronicle of the new wonder drug that has been said to "lend the introvert the social skills of a salesman" and, for some reason, the buttocks of a Romanian gymnast. The controversy begins when we start asking if it is a moral and proper thing that we start reengineering personalities—and for those who doubt if we should, let me just say two words: Shannen Doherty. My question to you, Dr. Kramer: Some people have committed suicide while on this drug—are there any other long-term side effects we should know about?

• • •

"If the Manson family had taken Prozac instead of speed and acid, today they'd be Fleetwood Mac."

—Bill

SOMEBODY'S GOTTA SAY IT

In Praise of Drugs

First aired 10·10·93

In the last ten years in America, drugs have gotten a bad name. That's mostly because the headlines go to the people who screw up with them, and then the whole class has to stay after. The truth is, anything you overdo or do wrong will make you sick. Food can kill you if you do too much of it. If you weigh a thousand pounds, maybe a little cocaine is just what you need. Not that I'm advocating cocaine—but I am advocating the belief that everyone in America is a different individual, and different in no place more incontrovertibly than their own physical chemistry, and that what may be a dangerous drug to you may not be a dangerous drug to me, and vice versa. Because it's not like the government forbids citizens from doing drugs—they have their list, and I don't know why their list is better than my list. Why is Halcion—which is banned in most countries and which caused one of our presidents to throw up on a Japanese prime minister—why is *that* drug and Valium and liquor legal, but not marijuana or mushrooms? Why did God make so many different kinds of mushrooms, and then one kind that's *really* different? I mean, when one species of mushroom is perfect for a cream sauce, and another for an omelette, and then there's one that makes you laugh for eight straight hours—that doesn't seem random to me. I believe God wanted us to laugh for eight straight hours

199

sometimes, because God knows life sucks. In the Bible, Job says to God, "God, why is there suffering? Can't you take away misery?" And God says, "No. Of course not, don't be silly. If I took away misery, no one would talk to me. But here's what I'll do: I'll give you drugs." This, of course, is a paraphrasing of God's sentiments—which I read in *The New Yorker*. Nevertheless, God did make a rather perfect world, and it seems positively sacrilegious to question His hand in the creation of any form of life, including herbs that induce giddiness as well as insight and creativity. Drug *abuse* is a horrible problem, but drug use—well, let's just say it didn't hurt my record collection. Doing stupid drugs or doing any drug stupidly *is* an abuse of your body. But a case could also be made for a type of mind abuse that ignores natural means put on the earth to expand mental vistas. If it's true that the most interesting place you can ever travel is inside your own head, then some people just never leave home.

The **Fairer Sex** —*or are* **They?**

Two lovable assholes.

Convenient Feminism |

First aired 9·19·93

Roseanne, Matt Lauer, Lorraine Bracco, John O'Sullivan

If you were on a sinking ship and yelled, "Women and children first!" how much feminist opposition do you think you'd get? Though claiming to be feminists, don't many women—when it suits them, when it's convenient—retreat back to their pre-feminist role of manipulating men through helpless, deferential behavior? Women want to fight men for equal pay, but how often do they fight a man for the check? They want an unlimited role in the military, but would they subject themselves to the draft if it were reinstated? And any man who questions a woman's physical capabilities gets branded a sexist—but who do they call when there's a spider to be killed? Convenient feminism—crackpot theory or dangerous lunacy?

• • •

"Who's superior, men or women? Women don't start wars or pollute oceans. But men don't throw crying fits and lock themselves in the bathroom when one of their friends gets married."
　　　　　　　　　　　　　　　—Bill

• • •

"I don't think women want to be equal to men. I think we'd have to have lobotomies to do that."
　　　　　　　　　　　　　　　—Roseanne

• • •

"When they say women and children first, they mean to go over-board and die."

—Roseanne

• • •

"You'd think we have some meetings. Have you ever been to a meeting, like, where we decided all this stuff?"

—Bill
(to Matt Lauer re a statement
made by Roseanne about men
making all the rules)

"No, because those meetings happen in those little enclaves where only males are allowed to go, and you know why they go there, without, well, you know why women are not allowed to go into those places—because that is where the males all dress up like women and have sex with each other."

—Roseanne

Date Rape |

First aired 11·5·93

Lisa Sliwa, Jonathan Katz, David Cassidy, R. Emmett Tyrrell

"Date rape" has become a dangerous blanket term that lies folded neatly at the foot of a burning bed. When a man and woman have sex, what constitutes consent? And can that consent, once given, be retracted? Recently, Antioch College forcibly inserted into its curriculum a campus sex code that makes giving women the upper hand Job One, and stiffly penalizes violators. At Antioch, before any sex may occur, there must be a formal verbal request from the man, a formal verbal agreement from the woman, and, surprisingly, the expressed, written consent of Major League Baseball. For some, this load of oral sanctions is a lot to swallow. Hasn't "date rape" become a catchall for sexual revisionist history, and, worse, hasn't it diluted the meaning of the horrid crime that is rape?

• • •

"Everywhere you go now, you have to ask, 'Can I put my hand up your shirt?' Then, 'Can I put my hand down your pants?' Of course, here in New York, that's usually the time you say, 'I'm sorry, I thought you were a girl!' "

—Bill

No Doesn't Mean No

First aired 10·3·93

Roseanne, Roger Clinton, Alexandra Penney, Richard Viguerie

Women do many things that men find contradictory, like displaying an ample cleavage and then getting mad at us when we look. Sorry, next time cut the top of your head off, and I'll stare at your brain. And then there's sex. We know that women like it as much as we do, but a woman can't just say yes to any possible sexual situation, because she'd then be—well, she'd be a man. And then where would we be? We'd all be gay, so that's out. But women do want it—which is why no sometimes just means "What do you think I am? Some kind of cheesy slut you can have for a quick glass of wine and a Caesar salad? Pony up a steak." Despite all the argle bargle about the new man and the new woman, the mating dance goes on much as it always has, and that includes the fact that no doesn't always mean no. Does anyone have a problem with that?

· · ·

"I think no woman should go outside of her home without a machine gun."

—Roseanne

Fired for Beauty

First aired 3·14·94

**Kelsey Grammer, Cynthia Heimel,
Bruce Herchensohn, Ruth Seymour**

Several celebrated court cases in the last few years, most notably involving flight attendants and female news anchors, have highlighted women's indignation at being fired for the crime of growing less attractive. But consider the opposite situation: a woman so beautiful that her mere presence distracts her boss from doing a lick of work. What's a guy to do? He doesn't want to sexually harass anybody, he tries to keep his nose in the actuarial tables—or say he's a surgeon, he tries to keep his nose in the patient's liver, but every time Nurse Pouty Breasts hands him a retractor, he just goes all thumbs . . . and then the patient dies. Now, who's fault is that? The question is, can a person be justifiably fired for being too beautiful?

Women Who Sleep to the Top

First aired 4·22·94

**Maureen Reagan, Dr. Joyce Brothers,
Jimmy Breslin, Richard Belzer**

Sexual harassment is one of the juicy issues that fascinate Americans, and for good reason: It tastes great and it's less filling. But seriously, it's gotten so much press because a lot of women have been harassed and a lot of men have done it. After seeing what happened to Clarence Thomas and Bob Packwood, men are thinking twice about doing anything that could be misinterpreted, like making off-color jokes or trying the popcorn trick during a slide presentation. This caution is fine, except it leaves out one important segment of people: What about women who *want* to sleep their way to the top? Feminists would disown them, but a desire to sleep with powerful, attractive men, like the president or a talk show host, should not, I say, be judged—and I think I can count on the support of Miss Marla Maples for this one. Women complain that men don't fight fair in the workplace, so here's a way they can fight not fair back. Does anybody have a problem with that?

• • •

"I'm against women sleeping their way to the top, but I'm all for letting a girl heavy-pet her way to middle management."
 —Bill

• • •

"How could women want to sleep with one of these guys, have you seen them? If the guy was sitting at a bar, and he was a woman, he wouldn't get his cigarette lit ..."

—Jimmy Breslin
(on bosses)

Women Hate Each Other

First aired 2·11·94

**Erica Jong, Jo Jo Starbuck,
Marcia Tucker, Angela Scott**

Pick up any issue of *Cosmopolitan,* and the first thing you'll usually notice on the cover are tantalizing blurbs like "How to Get to the Top—by Hitting Others with Pipe." My take on that? Chicks hate each other. For example, in New York, model Shaydie Sori teaches a seminar called "How to Steal a Man," which won't happen to me because I wear the Club. And if you ask a woman for the first word that comes to mind when she sees another attractive, sexy, provocative woman, the honest answer is usually "slut" or "whore" or even "Madonna." The feminist claim of a sisterhood is as bogus as the Mafia calling itself a brotherhood, and, especially when the disputed territory is a man, someone's gonna wind up wearing cement pumps at the bottom of the Yeast River. Women hate each other—does anyone have a problem with that?

· · ·

"Happy Valentine's Day. Today is a special day. A day to send that special someone chocolates, candy hearts, and perfume, to let her know you think of her as a fat person with cavities who smells."

—Bill

Women Are Vicious, Too

First Aired 1·7·94

Al Franken, Alan Dershowitz, Maureen O'Boyle, Armstrong Williams

For many men, the terms "feminism" and "women's libera-tion" still bring back memories of such militant actions as bra burning—which perhaps never had the effect women hoped for, since getting women out of their bras had been one of our goals for centuries. Now, in the nineties, there's been a change of tactics. The new trend is called "difference feminism," which takes as its basis Ashley Montagu's claim that, given the opportunity, women would humanize the world; that by their very nature, women are morally superior caregivers who pro-mote cooperation over cutthroat competition. Maybe so, but that wasn't exactly a Candy-Gram that Janet Reno sent to David Koresh this year in Texas. And talk about competition, what about the cheerleader mom from the same state? Okay, forget Texas—everyone in Texas is nuts. But Hillary Clinton isn't from Texas. And neither was Margaret Thatcher or Indira Gandhi or Madonna or, for that matter, Barney Frank. The point is, now that women are finally getting a chance to be on top, they're proving that they can be every bit as vicious and violent and hateful as men, and, boy, that really turns me on.

· · ·

"Linda Bloodworth-Thomason forced Delta Burke off of Designing Women. *The good news is she's returning to TV this fall as Perry Mason."*

—Bill

Hillary vs. Nancy

First aired 1·24·95

**Ken Hamblin, Bob Costas,
Lynn Snowden, Michael Deaver**

In 1989, Barbara Bush was disinvited by the women of Wellesley College from speaking at their graduation because these women felt that Mrs. Bush, with her traditional approach to being a wife, did not accurately reflect the more modern approach to power and access by women. As most of these Wellesley students were not married, Mrs. Bush could have probably told them a thing or two about who really controls decisions in a marriage, and she could have done it with two words: "Nancy Reagan." And if she were speaking today, those two words might also be "Hillary Clinton." Hillary and Nancy have a lot in common— they're both smarter than their husbands, and both consulted the stars for guidance, Nancy with astrology and Hillary with Barbra Streisand. The question is, which really makes a woman more powerful: Nancy Reagan's Helen Gurley Brown approach of manipulative feminine wiles behind the scenes, or Hillary's approach of just busting nuts?

• • •

"Hillary believes the health industry is a cancer, and Nancy has always thought of it as a Virgo."

—Bill

Kids *aren't* People *too*

SOMEBODY'S GOTTA SAY IT

No-Children Section

First aired 2·25·94

Americans long ago fell in love with the concept of rights, and that includes the right to squabble over whose rights are more important, your rights or my rights. It used to be my right to smoke a cigarette anywhere I damn well pleased, but nonsmokers organized and fought and captured that flag. So, good for them. But the truth is, America causes cancer. It's in every unnatural product and process and place in our lives, so to pick out one noxious fume among the hundreds we imbibe each day probably won't change the statistics all that much. Which is fine, except if we're going to get huffy about people doing things that annoy us, let's not be so selective about it.

Someone—let's say me—might enjoy cigarettes, but not children. Does that make me bad? I think it just makes me different, and not all that different. Plenty of people would rather have a cigarette than a child, and it's about time we stood up and demanded no-children sections just like they have no-smoking sections in restaurants and airplanes, because a screaming baby on the Continental red-eye is as hard on everybody's heart and blood pressure as two packs of Luckys. Don't make me get the statistics, because there are none, which is ridiculous. If they study the effects of secondhand smoke, they should study the effects of second-hand screaming and bratty behavior.

They say everybody loves kids, but that's wrong. Everybody loves their *own* kids. I don't like your kids any more than you like my cigarettes. In fact, your kids are the reason I smoke. A parent shares their child's joy and pain; I just get the pain. And children under two years old? They act like such . . . well, babies. Like screaming and crying is really a way to solve your problems. When I see how a child under two years old is behaving, I just want to say to him, "Grow up. Just grow up." Even churches once had crying rooms, and I think we well know that the Church loves its kids—sometimes a little too much. But it only seems fair that if I can put out my cigarette, you can tell your kid to shut up. Because if you don't tell your kid to shut up, the next time, when you're not looking, I'm gonna give him a cigarette.

License Parenthood

First aired 8·15·93

**Dr. Wilbert A. Tatum, Jane Pratt,
Ted Nugent, Martin Mull**

What do fishing, hunting, driving, and getting married have in common, beside the fact that they're all more fun when you're drunk? The real answer is, you need a license for all of them. But even though these activities are so tightly regulated, anyone can pick up a penis anytime they want and have a baby. Now, parenting has got to be a little more complicated than handling a car, with the possible exception of driving here in Manhattan. But given all the horror stories we hear about parents these days—leaving their kids home alone over Christmas or getting divorced by them—isn't it time we seriously considered licensing parenthood?

• • •

"Should we require a seven-day waiting period for having a child, and, if so, would it be called the Brady Bunch Bill?"
 —Bill

The Younger, Wimpy Generation

First aired 9·5·93

**Joy Behar, Moon Zappa,
Jay Severin, Sy Sperling**

It's been said that if you're not a radical at twenty, you have no heart; but if you're still a radical at forty, you have no brain. Of course, either way, at sixty you usually have no teeth. A democracy depends on a loyal opposition questioning the values of the ruling class, and the spirit of that opposition usually comes from the youth. However, in the last ten years the biggest protest song recorded has been "You've Got to Fight for Your Right to Party," which is not exactly "Blowin' in the Wind." The sixties generation said, "Give peace a chance." This generation says, "Give sushi a chance." Isn't the failure to rebel a black mark on the current generation, and shouldn't they feel like shallow, limp mama's boys who'd be lucky to get a parking ticket overturned?

• • •

"If Leave It to Beaver *was done in the nineties, Beaver would have a crack problem and Wally would be dating Lumpy."*
 —Bill

SOMEBODY'S GOTTA SAY IT

The Spur Posse

First aired 6·14·94

Twenty-year-old Dana Bellman is handsome, athletic, and popular, and he's also the founder of the Spur Posse, a gang of sporting, strapping suburban locals who awarded each other points for, at best, coerced sex and, at worst, rape with girls as young as ten. But it's not like the Spur Posse don't have their supporters, among them Dana's father, Don Belman, who said of his sons, "Aren't they virile specimens?" Then there's posse member Billy Sheehan, who said, "We didn't do nothing wrong," possibly not realizing his grammatical lapse. You know how kids are: One minute they're dropping a consonant, the next minute, rape. They grow up so fast, and apparently without any moral instruction.

It's easy to blame society for this one—American culture floods young boys with images of sexual conquest and violence as the golden measure of masculinity. Mike Tyson—who is guilty of rape—is no worse than a controversial figure, and Magic Johnson is a downright hero, as we conveniently forget that he didn't get AIDS from singing too loud in the choir. Of course, I'm not against hooker threesomes, but for you kids out there, maybe you shouldn't try this at home.

They had sex scandals in Fatty Arbuckle's day too, but the difference today is the parenting. What values are taught when a father is proud of his son for being in the Spur Posse? Kids do cruel and stupid things, and fathers are sup-

posed to tell them not to. That's the father's job, to teach them something. Mr. Bellman, you seem like the kind of guy who watched the Republican convention last year, with all that talk about "family values," and here's your chance to make Marilyn Quayle proud. Family values—it's not complicated. You have a family, teach them some values.

Trophy Syndrome

First aired 12·5·93

**Martin Mull, Joe Queenan,
Henry Rollins, Dr. Joyce Brothers**

Imagine a world where you can't use the word "bad." Imagine a world where the spelling mistakes of school children aren't corrected, for fear it will "stifle their creativity," and school boards eliminate student rankings. Imagine a world where pixies beat pretty tunes in your ears with the fluttering of their wings, and dogs crap chocolate ice cream. Well, it's all true. Okay, except for the pixies and the dogs. It's part of something in America called the "self-esteem movement," and it aims to shower praise on kids every time they cross a room without killing themselves. But, in so doing, isn't it killing their chances to grow up strong?

• • •

"I just got the Playboy Channel—for the articles."
—Bill

Kids—Young Adults

First aired 4·8·94

Sen. Arlen Specter, Gloria Allred, John Waters, Sarah Jessica Parker

As more and more of our most violent crimes are now committed by young offenders, measures are being taken to bring about some semblance of control, like that sign in gun shops that says YOU MUST BE THIS TALL TO PURCHASE A WEAPON. Because children are beloved, America has not had the stomach to face up to the fact that kids are a big part of the crime problem and that twelve-year-olds no longer fit the outdated image we cling to. They're too well informed to be innocent, too well armed to be ignored, too ruthless to be excused, and, most tragically, too sexy for their shirts. The point is, a two-year-old in 1994 is probably more like what a twenty-year-old was in 1954. So the question is, doesn't it make sense to rethink our notion of "age of responsibility" and stop letting today's kids get away with murder?

• • •

"I know a kid, he can't be more than seven or eight, and I asked him if he knew about the birds and the bees. He said, 'I can only assume they make it like people do.' "

—Bill

• • •

"When I was a child and we heard the Road Runner go beep, beep, we used to get hysterical. Now the kids hear it, and they check their pagers."

—Bill

Sarah Jessica Parker, Sen. Arlen Specter, Gloria Allred, John Waters:
They've all gone on to be good friends.

If We Teach Homo, Why Not Necro or Lamb?

First aired 12·18·93

**Jill Brooke, Pat Cooper,
Michael Medved, Michael Lewis**

New York City Schools Chancellor Joseph Fernandez recently lost his job because he supported a curriculum designed to teach respect for diversity, including homosexuality, in the public schools. The reading list for the program included such page-turners as *Heather Has Two Mommies* and *Daddy Has a Roommate.* Some parents and school board members objected to what they perceived as an endorsement of homosexuality as a lifestyle choice, since this curriculum seemed to open the door for any number of groups to claim the same privilege. Prostitutes might suggest a book called *Heather Has 350 Daddies* and practicers of bestiality might ask for one called *Heather, Run out and Get Mommy Some Woolite.* American schools haven't exactly been breaking records in teaching our kids how to read and write—aren't they a little over their heads with this one?

• • •

"In New York now they have Harvey Milk High School for gay students. They don't have much of a football team, but the half-time show . . ."

—Bill

Use Up Orphans

First aired 3·4·94

**Bob Somerby, Lynn Martin,
Letitia Baldrige, Gene Siskel**

When someone wants a dog, we all advise him to do the right thing and go to the pound to save a hapless orphan of the storm. But when it comes to people, we often overlook a simple solution—Mia Farrow. The infertility problem has given birth to an inconceivable number of wacky solutions like test-tube babies, surrogate mothers, and cloning, which really scares me because I can't even handle the Olson twins. The point is, our instincts are right on the money when it comes to dogs. All methods of phony procreation should be banned until we use up the orphans we already have. Does anybody have a problem with that?

• • •

"Some people are far too old to be having kids. I saw this ad the other night with this poor old woman screeching, 'Help, I've fallen and I can't get knocked up.' "

• • •

"So many adopted kids search for their parents. Hey, take a hint!"

—Bill

Restore the Rod

First aired 1·14·93

Bob Somerby, Tama Janowitz, Paul Kramer, James "The Amazing" Randi

The New York Times Magazine recently described how a class of third-graders wanted to sue their teacher for making them write apologies after a big fight. Unfortunately, the kids couldn't find an attorney who'd work for milk money. But the point is, in an age of nonexistent supervision and nonstop television, kids have become mini-adults, and the real adults are afraid to pull rank. That's because nowadays, if you have any physical contact with a kid, you're either accused of hitting him—or hitting *on* him. Now, I'm not suggesting the kind of brutal discipline found in certain radical cults, like the Catholics, but isn't it time parents stopped negotiating with their children and just told them to shut the hell up?

• • •

"Kids today are out of control. E.T. told Drew Barrymore at the end of the movie to be a good girl. Boy, is he going to be surprised when he comes back."

—Bill

Child Molesters and Nuclear Power Plants

First aired 10·27·94

Well, it's Halloween again, the time of year when we're supposed to be frightened by unreal and fantastical creatures like goblins and ghouls. The problem in the modern world, however, is that there are much more scary creatures in reality. Yes, *Frankenstein* is a scary story, but if you really want a chill, think about Frankenstein's modern counterpart—today's sex offender. He also roams the countryside and terrorizes townspeople, but he's hardly misunderstood, and that big, scary zipper isn't on his neck.

Several recent cases have sparked debate over where to put sex offenders who've done their time and paid their debt to society. The problem is, on the one hand, everyone deserves a second chance in life—even if they're not running for mayor of Washington—but, on the other hand, no one wants dangerous men roaming the countryside looking to prey on children. After all, we've got Boy Scouts leaders for that.

In a sense, sex offenders are viewed something like nuclear power plants: Everyone knows we need to put them somewhere, but no one wants them in their own backyard. Which leads to an obvious and entirely practical solution: Make the child molesters live near the nuclear power plants. The fact is, we have to put them somewhere, and what sex

offender wouldn't want to live in a town called Love Canal? This way, we can neatly group together anything that's liable to leak fluid. More to the point, shouldn't nuclear plants be staffed by guys who already have plenty of experience handling contaminated waste and spent rods?

In short, this is a win-win situation: Given the makeup of the town and the dangers of radioactivity, abstinence will be a compelling lifestyle choice. Even sex offenders don't want to join the Three Mile Island club!

Holidays

on thin

Ice

Walk-in Closet

First aired 10·11·94

Gay Talese, Michael Musto, Suzanne Westenhoefer, Pat Dinizio

Today is National Coming Out Day, when homosexual celebrities are supposed to come out of the closet and, if they see their shadow, we know there'll be six more weeks of the Barbra Streisand tour. For years now, gay rights advocates have urged these stars to reveal themselves in order to better ensure that homosexuality never again be seen as something to hide or be ashamed of—not to mention make it easier to tell who's available Saturday night. But is this pressure really fair? If voting and praying are guaranteed privacy by the United States Constitution, why not the most private of acts, screwing?

How the Grinches Stole Halloween

Show aired 10·27·94

**John Waters, Rep. Susan Molinari,
Scott Baio, Melissa Etheridge**

Time was when Halloween was a great holiday, a night when kids could roam the streets alone and not get suspicious when a grown-up asked them to go bobbing for apples. But lately, the very idea of Halloween has been stolen by a host of real-life grinches. Like in Iowa, where schools have decided that "Halloween" is too scary, so they now call it the "Harvest Festival." For the same reason, Easter is now known as "Jesus Takes a Nap." Elsewhere, Halloween has been body-snatched as a Gay Liberation Day, which undermines the notion that a holiday is supposed to be a truce; using it to promote political agendas is like putting a razor blade in an apple. So I say it's time to turn Halloween into what it used to be—an amusing holiday for the kids. Anyone have a problem with that?

. . .

"I've lived in New York and Los Angeles and, in those cities on Halloween, you're either gay or you're watching."
—Bill

. . .

"I always feel sorry for people in Halloween costumes. You notice when they're going home drunk, alone, and you see them at like two in the morning in a rabbit costume waiting for a bus. It's so sad."

<div align="right">

—John Waters

</div>

GET OVER YOURSELF

Santa

First aired 12·20·94

Once again, it's time for our Prince Rogers Nelson "Get Over Yourself" Award.

So far this year we've given the award to a wide array of deserving egomaniacs—people like Lance Ito, Mickey Rourke, Newt Gingrich, Howard Stern, and, of course, Prince himself. But this week the award goes to the person who deserves it most of all—a man who drives a sleigh, but who has been getting a free ride for much too long. When Santa Claus first burst on the scene, he seemed a little too good to be true: Everyone in America was going to be personally delivered a bag of gifts—and all on the same day, no less? Even Clinton doesn't make promises like that.

But Santa Claus—or, as people started to call him, "Santa"—made good on his promise, and made some nice goods. But even though everything seemed fine on the surface, it wasn't. Goodwill toward men, yes, but what about elves? It's a cute name, but there's nothing cute about slave labor. And I guess, in the fifties, we were so paranoid about Communism that the idea of a guy making a list of everyone who was naughty or nice didn't seem so scary, but it's an anachronism now, and it's offensive.

Almost as offensive as the animal abuse issue. My God, going around the world in one night is a job for eighty reindeer, not eight—or actually seven now. A few years ago Blitzen had a heart attack over Greenland; it was covered up, but it's

true—Blitzen is dead, he's in a Jewish cemetery in Canada. Meanwhile, we let this abusive, overeating cross-dresser hold court in a mall and we willingly send our children to sit on his lap. Santa, Saint Nick, Kris Kringle, whatever name you're using this week—it's over for you, pal. *It's* over, so why don't you get over yourself?

A MODEST PROPOSAL

Bachelor Day

First aired 2·11·94

Valentine's Day is upon us, and of course this is the day when everyone in the world should be in love. Yeah, *should* be, just like everyone *should* be healthy and *should* be rich.

The problem with planet Earth, however, is that being "in love" is something that comes along infrequently and then doesn't last, and in its place are two inferior options— loneliness and marriage. Take marriage—please. It's a necessary evil, because loneliness is intolerable and behaving like Aerosmith just isn't allowed in most states. So we pair up with one person, and crush any hope of remaining undeadened to our partner by piling upon each other a ridiculous number of responsibilities—lover, best friend, co-parent, fitness advisor, dinner companion.

But let's be frank. The real problem with marriage is that it's just very difficult to bump your uglies with the same person every night your whole life. I may like toast, I may think toast is the most perfect food there is—and I do think that of toast—but I don't only eat toast. The thought of total monogamy for a lifetime becomes an unbearable psychological burden, but it could be eased if America would only consider this very modest proposal: Bachelor Day. A new holiday that comes once a year, on the former Flag Day, which is now wiped out because no one ever gave a rat's ass.

Bachelor Day would be the best thing for the institution of marriage. Every year, on June 14, during that lovely week

when horny spring is metamorphosing into sultry summer, every married person in America, by executive order of the president—and wouldn't he love to sign this one?—every married person on June 14 is given a one-day furlough from his or her marital responsibilities. This would serve to purge all that pent-up curiosity and boredom that undermines a union while allowing the participants to play within the rules. Just imagine reliving the excitement and anticipation of your prom—every year—without the worry of messing up the backseat of your dad's car.

Of course, in most cases, this naughty little tryst will just make the participants even more appreciative of their real partners. So you see, it is a sweet, Valentine-like thing. And Hallmark will prove that with their "Get Laid Soon" card in May, and their "Congratulations, You Finally Did Her" in July. In fact, Bachelor Day is not only good for relationships, it would be a huge commercial boon for the national economy. Bookings for hotels, motels, and rental cars would skyrocket, as would the sale of condoms, flowers, French ticklers, chocolates, alcohol, scented jellies, whipped cream, cigarettes, and Crisco.

What could be better, or more quintessentially American, than screwing our way to a better economy? Bachelor Day—it's coming.

No Stress Compensation

First aired 6·14·94

**Maureen Reagan, Dr. Joyce Brothers,
Jimmy Breslin, Richard Belzer**

Are you tired of working but not sick enough to quit? Have you ever snapped on the job and wanted to kill a coworker but didn't because it would just increase your workload? Well, for increasing numbers of Americans, these questions never come up because they can collect workers' compensation simply by crying "stress." The problem is, telling your boss you don't want to work because of stress is like telling your spouse you don't want to have sex because you're married. Work *is* stress—that's what they're paying you for. That's why people don't get up and go to "fun" in the morning, and that's why carpenters don't say "put that drill on my funbench." If your job is getting to be too much for you, sell the BMW and get an easier job, but don't go bleating to the government because you've got claw marks on the inside of your aspirin bottle. Does anyone have a problem with that?

• • •

"I just read that when the Dalai Lama works too hard, he relaxes by watching reruns of M*A*S*H. *That's ironic because when McLean Stevenson gets uptight about working too much . . . well, I guess he doesn't have that problem."*

—Bill

Below *the* Bible

Belt

A MODEST PROPOSAL

Put a Warning Label on the Bible

First aired 10·8·93

As America has become increasingly violent, there are those who have suggested such outlandish and preposterous measures as gun control, honest police departments, and comprehensive drug treatment as ways of dealing with the problem. Luckily, the good sense of Americans has prevailed and we have all agreed on the one solution that dispatches violence most effectively: warning labels. The television industry made headlines this year when the networks finally agreed to carry viewer advisories before some of their shows, following the lead of the music industry, which for some years now has been slapping cautionary stickers on any record that might make people want to kill themselves, not including Fleetwood Mac. In addition, family associations in hundreds of towns across America have lately been alerting their citizens to the dangers inherent in hundreds of books, including works by William Faulkner, Maya Angelou, and even Dr. Seuss.

But if you really want to crack down on books that inspire violence, there's one book that far more than any other cries out for a warning label: the Bible. David Koresh is only the most recent example of a violent zealot who based his insanity on what he read in the Scriptures. Michael Griffin shot and killed an abortion doctor with the words, "I did it because I love Jesus"—the things people do to gain that man's approval. But Griffin has plenty of com-

pany: Jim Jones to John Brown to Klan wizards to Cotton Mather, citing the Bible is almost de rigeur before any crackpot goes loco in the modern world, to say nothing of the Crusades. Even David Berkowitz, the Son of Sam killer, heard voices from a dog. Berkowitz, of course, was dyslexic.

Now the fault, of course, does not lie within the Bible itself, which most people see as filled with peace and faith, but rather with man's unlimited capacity for misinterpretation. I assume that's why the makers of Easy Off consider it necessary to write big letters on the can discouraging us from swallowing the stuff. But Easy Off never started a war or got someone burned at a stake, so at the very least I propose that the Bible carry a sticker that says, "Warning: This volume may cause a desire to smite infidels, fondle church secretaries, or separate poor old people from their welfare checks. Read with caution." Oh, and one other thing: It should also say, "This book should not be taken internally."

Medical Vietnam

First aired 3·10·95

**Hillary B. Smith, Jimmy Aleck,
Charles Bierbauer, Dr. Bernie Siegel**

Recently a Virginia court ruled that a hospital had to keep alive a baby born with most of its brain missing, even though it was costing taxpayers fifteen hundred dollars a day. The argument for keeping this baby alive is obvious— he could be the next host of *Family Feud*—but with the war over health care costs heating up, shouldn't public dollars be saved for procedures that improve the quality of life for everyone, like breast implants? Sure, someone in a persistent vegetative state is technically alive—just look at Strom Thurmond—but in an age of limits, we have to come to grips with the fact that the gift of life simply cannot be indulged for everything with a heartbeat. Does anybody have a problem with that?

• • •

"It costs taxpayers hundreds of thousands of dollars to keep brain-dead Americans alive each year. These costs could be cut in half if we were just allowed to sell some of their stuff."
—Bill

Roger Clinton: Poor guy, always afraid his brother is going to embarrass him.

Tax the Church?

First aired 10·3·93

**Roseanne, Roger Clinton,
Alexandra Penney, Richard Viguerie**

The Catholic Church has always had some curious notions about sex, dating back to the time the Church denied Henry VIII permission to divorce Anne Boleyn. At that point, Henry threatened to behead her, to which the Church, of course, responded, "No problem. Beheading's fine, it's just divorce that makes us nervous." More recently, Archbishop Robert Sanchez of Santa Fe was appalled to learn that David Koresh was sleeping with young girls in Waco, Texas, because, after all, in Santa Fe, the priests were sleeping with boys *and* girls. Sanchez got a cozy twenty minutes with Mike Wallace, while Koresh got a flaming Candy-Gram from the FBI. My question is, isn't a religion just a cult that doesn't have to pay taxes, and shouldn't it pay them?

Hypothetical Pope

First aired 10·19·94

**Joe Queenan, Harry Smith,
E. Jean Carroll, Joe Bolster**

This has been a disappointing October for sports fans, first with no World Series and then with the pope cancelling his visit to Giants Stadium, thus depriving us of the first concert to feature Cardinal O'Connor in a mosh pit. One billion Catholics around the world look to the pope for spiritual guidance, secular leadership, and honest advice on car repair, but the question remains: What makes this guy an authority on sex, anyway? If any other celibate old despot said that you couldn't masturbate, use birth control, or have sex whenever you wanted, he'd be run out of town. Religious beliefs should be private and sacred, but in an age when AIDS and overpopulation threaten to decimate the planet, I say that abiding anyone's advice against using condoms or birth control is an indulgence that the human race can no longer afford. Does anyone have a problem with that?

· · ·

"I'm the oldest of fourteen children. My mom worked on a commission basis for the pope."

—Joe Bolster

· · ·

"You have these nuns beating your knuckles bloody and then telling you they were the sisters of God, and I felt like, 'I don't want to meet your brother.' "

—Joe Bolster

. . .

"I'm not Catholic, but aren't all Catholics afraid of the pope? We used to play basketball behind the Catholic school, we were afraid to go in the Catholic church there. There are scary things in there—there are big women in black clothes with rulers who run around beating on people all the time . . ."

—Harry Smith

"That's also on the back of certain magazines you can buy here in New York."

—Bill

. . .

"The Catholic Church is sort of like the National Hockey League. You go away for twenty years, the rules never change."

—Joe Queenan

Life and Death

First aired 11·19·93

A man recently sued a hospital for saving his life. He wanted to die after suffering a heart attack and the hospital went ahead and saved him anyway without even asking. Boy, talk about nerve. There was also a "wrongful birth" suit filed by the parents of a failed vasectomy, and, of course, everywhere in America there is bitter, bloody conflict over abortion, the death penalty, and euthanasia.

All of which brings up the question, are there any two people in this country anymore who agree on life and death? And even more fundamentally, isn't this an area where God had pretty much always said to man, "Hey, if I want your opinion I'll kill you and ask you when you get up here"? And yet, matters of life and death now seem to many an apposite place for partisan politics—not that I can even figure out where the partisans line up. Take abortion, for example. It seems to me that pro-choice should be a *conservative* position. Conservatives are for unrestricted choice in everything: what school you can go to, what doctor you can pick, who you can pal around with. "Get the government off the people's back," Ronald Reagan said—but apparently in their uterus is okay.

Of course, what I really don't understand is why conservative fundamentalists defend the fringes of life so staunchly when the most basic tenet of religion is that life on earth is a trifling way-station on the road to a glorious hereafter. The

message from religion is "Hey, life's okay, but things really get good when you're dead." But if they really believe that, why make such a fuss about hanging on to life for unwanted fetuses and the terminally ill? It's easy for the young and healthy to say, "Life is precious, hang on to it." But how precious is it if you're ninety-five, drooling, and insane?

Sometimes it's just time to get off the stage before they get the cosmic hook. Really spiritual people like the Indians go up on a mountain somewhere when they're ready to die and pass on into the next world with acceptance and equanimity. The rest of us go to Miami and prepare for death by playing shuffleboard. Not that there's anything wrong with shuffleboard as a preparation for death, because after all, there probably is no way to really prepare for death, except to maintain the faith that in death, there awaits us something more noble and sublime than we've known on earth. And it seems to me that for anyone who really believes that, there would be a greater tolerance for the issues of life that now divide us so much on earth.

Field *of*
Nightmares

A MODEST PROPOSAL

Bread for the Bleachers

First aired 10·29·93

Well, baseball is finally over for another year, but here in New York, there's no rest for George Steinbrenner, who's threatening to sneak the Yankees out of Yankee Stadium for the same reason that many sports moguls have uprooted their teams in recent years: because their stadium couldn't accommodate skyboxes.

Skyboxes are those luxury condos within a stadium where the very rich can go and say they've been to a baseball game without having to actually watch it. Inside, they serve such traditional ballgame fare as oysters and champagne, and they have waitresses and even televisions, just in case you want to catch a ballgame. Skyboxes grant the rich the license to buy off bad weather, and now there are even skyboxes within domed stadiums, in case your entire immune system shuts down.

I'm sorry, but it's sickening that sports has become the indulgence of the idle rich. Watching baseball on TV used to be one of the last free pleasures available to the common man, and millions of people—poor people or shut-ins or just plain fans—could tune in their team every night, 162 games a year. Well, now a lot of those sporting events are on cable or pay-per-view, which is why they need the money for those skyboxes.

Not that the rich being obnoxious is anything new, but at least in ancient Rome, when the emperor and his privileged

elite watched the games from their skyboxes in the Coliseum, they took a little more responsibility in mollifying the masses. They gave them "bread and circuses," which is one loaf more than we're getting today. I mean, there's no denying they give us circuses—the Yankees are certainly a circus, to say nothing of the Mets and their Amazing Coleman, the "Fire Thrower," but where's the bread?

I say, if you're rich enough to be slurping shrimp cocktails at a baseball stadium that you blackmailed the city into building for you, then the least you could do is buy bread for the proletariat sitting in the bleachers. So, that's my plan: Bread for the Bleachers! Everyone sitting in the bleachers gets one loaf of bread upon entering the stadium—compliments of the skybox—and not the crappy white kind, either, but a decent loaf of bread, and maybe some sort of spread! Bread for the Bleachers—that's my solution to the sports problem.

Fans Get What They Deserve

First aired 6·10·94

**Lisa Jones, Roger Corman,
Dave Chappelle, Bob Costas**

When it comes to baseball, the debate over who's worse—
the players or the owners—may be the toughest call in the
game. For every Steinbrenner who thinks his ball club is just
a corporation made up of movable fences, ballparks, and
players, there's a Darryl Strawberry who'd rather stay in bed
with the sniffles—okay, really bad sniffles—and have his $4
million paycheck sent home. But what's being left out of the
equation is this: The fans suck, too. Eight years after Bill
Buckner made an error in the World Series, the good peo-
ple of New England were still giving him such crap that he
finally had to move his family to Utah. Players here in New
York are booed for playing under par when they're injured,
not to mention getting pelted in the outfield with the give-
aways from Fan Appreciation Day, and nowadays when a
team wins the championship, the "celebration" gets so out
of hand it brings new meaning to the term "die-hard fans."
And worst of all, there's those sticky soda puddles under the
seats. Owners suck, players suck, but fans suck, too. Does
anybody have a problem with that?

• • •

*"It's gotten so bad at baseball games that fans sit in the stands
getting drunk, smoking, and shouting racial slurs at players—
and that's just Marge Schott."*

—Bill

• • •

"I think that if you're not playing the game, and you don't own the team, you can only be so passionate—unless you've got gambling debts."

—Dave Chappelle

Sports Fans—Get a Life

First aired 10·4·94

**Bob Costas, Keith Hernandez,
Huey Lewis, Gabrielle Reece**

Well, it's October, and the baseball season is long gone, which is why fans everywhere are in a deep funk, and why, for the first time in months, Darryl Strawberry is peeing with confidence. Now, we all miss the World Series, but sometimes from a negative comes a positive, and in this case, that positive is perspective: Sports is pretend, and life is real, and if baseball were meant to be taken seriously, they wouldn't make Tommy Lasorda trot out in tight pants. I say, by breaking a bad addiction and reminding us of other little things, like relationships and reading, the baseball strike has done all Americans an invaluable service. Does anybody have a problem with that?

GET OVER YOURSELF

Deion Sanders

First aired 10·20·94

Well, it's time for this week's "Get Over Yourself" Award. Tonight's lucky recipient is a man whose influence is so great that he embodies literally everything that's wrong with sports today. When Deion Sanders was drafted out of college in both football and baseball, he said he wanted to do things even Bo Jackson hadn't done, and he did—if you count running a 4.5 40 dressed like Aunt Jemima on a jewelry spree. Deion has endlessly annoyed management and teammates, he's brought the art of taunting to undiscovered depths, and he spends more time on his hair than Hillary Clinton. Even worse, in an age of megastars who truly believe the earth *and* the sun revolve around them, "Neon Deion"—or "Prime Time," as he calls himself in his more reflective moments—is the quintessential free agent out for himself.

Deion, you've got truly wonderful athletic gifts, but they're *gifts,* so be *thankful.* Someday—maybe someday soon—they'll vanish, and so will all the attention. Meanwhile, I can *almost* forgive the time you dumped ice on Tim McCarver for having the gall to question your play; I can *almost* forgive you for calling the Georgia Dome "my house" when you don't even play there; but being friends with *Hammer?* Still, for me the final straw came in the 49ers-Falcons game last Sunday, when you high-stepped down the sideline with one hand on the ball and the other

behind your head like Rita Hayworth, mocking your old teammates and turning a thing of athletic beauty into an ugly display of hubris. For all that and more—Deion Sanders, get over yourself!

The Drug Olympics

First aired 2·25·94

Well, the Winter Olympics are here again this week, and I think all of us watching have the same reaction to the events: Okay, if you say these are actual sports, I guess I believe you, but I never actually saw anyone bobsledding or skiing over those big speed bumps in real life. But it's February, and it's sweeps month, and there's no good mini-series on, and the war in Bosnia isn't scheduled to start for another two weeks, so sure, we'll zone out on this for a while because it's too cold outside to argue about it or do anything else.

But the real problem with the Olympics now isn't the cold, it's the Cold War—it's over and with it went all our fervent rooting interest. Now, I appreciate the efforts of net-work marketing people to set up a chick fight between skaters so we'd stay amused and have *something* to root for, but that's still pretty tame stuff next to the Olympic proxy fight we had for forty years between us free-nation good guys and the Communist bad guys. Those were the days when we could cheer for our whole way of life, because that's what the Olympics always *was* during the Cold War, just a huge pissing match that said our very way of life is superior to your whole way of life, and nowhere will that be proven more conclusively than in lugeing.

Okay, it was silly, but it was better than actually going to war, and it did give us a lot of insight into our Cold War

enemies. If anybody had any doubt that the Russians would cheat on a missile treaty, all they had to do was look at the testicles on their women athletes. Which brings me around to steroids and growth hormones and whatever other medical breakthroughs these athletes obviously want so badly to use in their pursuit of quasi-human achievement. World records in the Olympics were once an occasion for celebrations, not allegations, but nowadays gold medals bring with them as much doubt as glory. And understandably so, because we never really know who's clean, and athletes who want to use performance-enhancing drugs will always find a way to beat the tests.

So why not let them? We need to revive Olympic interest, so now would be a good time to see how fast a guy could run the 100 meters with, say, four legs. And if the name of the event is speed skating, let's see some skating on speed. And really, with an event like the bobsled, how much phonier could it be if those guys were hopped up on goofballs and they just had a designated driver and three guys in the back laughing and screaming?

Not to mention what a boon legalizing drugs would be for many other countries. Bolivia would become very competitive, Turkey would be a force to reckon with, and the Jamaican bobsled team? Well, I guess they were always stoned anyway. But if nothing else moves you, think about that poor skier crashing on the beginning of *Wide World of Sports*. For once in his life, he might actually get a medal.

Things *we* want *to* Kill

Kill Marriage

First aired 8·1·93

**Tom Arnold, Victor Kiam,
Russ Hodge, Lisa Sliwa**

If two bottles of Excedrin turn up tampered with, the entire inventory gets recalled, and if a couple of GM pickups burst into flames, the next-of-kin start whining about a recall. But even though over 50 percent of the marriages in this country fail, nobody ever thinks that the model *there* might be faulty. Given all the changes in society since marriage began, plus the fact that those incredible chicks in the MTV videos are in your face twenty-four hours a day, is this institution the only idea we can come up with for people who love each other?

. . .

"Today we're going to talk about marriage. But only in the most general, theoretical terms, and we're not making any commitments."

—Bill

. . .

"The only guns they should allow are the kind from the old days, from when they wrote the Constitution when where, you know, you're mad at someone, you gotta get your gun, get a ball of steel, you put the powder in it; you know, by the time you're done, it's over."

—Tom
(on gun control)

• • •

"To me it's like, I think of you, 'cause you had a football team. The same thing with football; we want the football players, we want to see them on game day hyped up to this macho frenzy. We don't want to see them in . . ."

—Bill
(to Victor Kiam, former owner of the New England Patriots, comparing football players with the military in the Tailhook scandal)

"You never saw his team."

—Tom Arnold

Kill Evil

First aired 8·29·93

**Larry Miller, Joe Queenan,
Vinette Pryce, Mark Katz**

Manuel Noriega was a drug dealer who enslaved his country, so we invaded and arrested him. Iraq invaded Kuwait and threatened our oil supply, so we invaded and threw them out, *and,* more importantly, made Mr. and Mrs. Blitzer proud they named their son Wolf. My question is, with characters like Noriega and Saddam Hussein who've put the "dict" back in "dictator," why all the handwringing about the legality of invasion and other such argle-bargle? Where evil is plain, don't we have a right to invade and kill it?

• • •

"A lot of people have warned President Clinton that Bosnia will turn into another Vietnam, which would be embarrassing for him because he'll have to go back to college."
—Bill

Kill Shrinks

First aired 10·4·93

**Andrea Martin, Garry Ross,
Tama Janowitz, Tony Snow**

Nowadays, because the rich and famous can afford to indulge themselves with psychiatry, the human mind gets a lot of press, but most people know that if the mind was really that entertaining, they'd have Professional Wrestling with an Idea. Psychiatry was originally intended for people who are really nuts, but now it's just degenerated into a lot of yuppies taking long lunch hours in a shrink's office so they can whine to some guy in a beard—or woman in a beard—about how they can't get laid or how they got locked in the closet with a spider when they were three. The problem is, these people are only digging up the inevitable traumas of childhood, which our own human, natural forces of oblivion work so hard to bury. Childhood is painful but the mind blocks out pain over time, so shouldn't we, in most cases, just leave that formula alone instead of trying to make money off of it?

• • •

"I'm not sure how qualified some psychiatrists are. My brother's psychiatrist once said to him, 'Maybe life isn't for everyone.'"
—Andrea Martin

• • •

"First of all, you can't find anyone to listen to you. I don't know about your friends, but my friends want to tell me their problems."
—Tama Janowitz

Kill the NEA

First aired 12·12·93

**Harry Shearer, Fran Drescher,
Sen. Eugene McCarthy, Rep. Bernie Sanders**

The difference between Democrats and Republicans, it might be said, is that at least the Democrats admit they're wasting your money, whereas the Republicans pretend they're saving it. The original idea of government was a pooling of resources to better ensure the survival of the tribe, which brings us to the National Endowment for the Arts, and would somebody please tell me what that has to do with survival? Putting food on the table is survival. Putting food on your breasts and genitals—well, I don't know much about art, but I know what I like. The point is, government should exist for only those fundamental undertakings that the private sector cannot provide. Does anyone have a problem with that?

• • •

"There is a difference between classic art at a museum and avant-garde art at a gallery. They serve wine at both, but at the museum, the cork is in the bottle. At the gallery, the cork is in the artist."

—Bill

Kill Polls

First aired 3·4·94

**Bob Somerby, Lynn Martin,
Letitia Baldridge, Gene Siskel**

Ed Rollins once said on this show that the only reason we even have elections is to see if the polls were right. Of course, he retracted it the next day. But the fact is, we're poll-happy in America: We've got Gallup, CBS, CNN, and *USA Today,* and here in Washington, even the vote for most popular kid in the class has a sampling error of plus or minus 3 percent. But the problem is, polls don't just predict elections, they determine them. Ross Perot could've become president if so many people hadn't been convinced that he was a wasted vote and if there wasn't that little thing about him being psychotic. The point is, when you step behind that curtain, the voting booth should be a sacred chamber for you and your conscience, but polls shove the rest of the country in with the voter and that's not a democracy, it's a shower scene. I say polling and reporting poll results should be illegal in America. Does anybody have a problem with that?

• • •

"A recent Washington Post *poll revealed that sixty percent of Americans approve of the president's performance, although women in the eighteen-to-twenty-five-year-old category wish he would last a little longer."*

—Bill

Kill Plea Bargains

First aired 4·15·94

**William Kunstler, Steve Allen,
Brett Butler, Donovan Leitch**

This week brought to an end the sad story of Chuck Jones, Marla Maples's former publicist whose only crime was loving his client's shoes too much and who gave a whole new meaning to the phrase "Does this come in a smaller size?" But Chuck's biggest mistake was not being shoe horny, it was having faith in the American system of justice. Instead of plea bargaining, Chuck went to trial and got four years of jail time, not to mention one hundred hours of court-appointed therapy from Dr. Scholl. In Oregon, the DA's office couldn't be bothered with getting to the bottom of the Tonya Harding case, so they let her plea bargain and skate away. And on Long Island, Joey Buttafuoco plea bargained and got off—or, rather, he got off and then plea bargained. The point is, prosecutors' offices have turned into Middle Eastern bazaars, where court officers haggle like rug merchants and justice is bartered like cigarettes in a prison yard, which is where most of the beneficiaries of plea bargaining belong.

• • •

"Chuck Jones was sentenced to four years in prison for having sex with Marla Maples's shoes. But the joke is on the judge, because he sent Chuck to boot camp."

—Bill

Kill Santa

First aired 10·4·93

Andrea Martin, William Kunstler, Bob Guccione, Jr., Roger Stone

Children today are forced, by the fierce and yeasty tenor of our times to grow up much faster than they ever did before, which brings us to the problem of Santa Claus. Santa is a problem because he does nothing but set kids up for being disillusioned. In fact, it may be time for Santa Claus to retire, considering that these days if a big fat old dude in a red suit actually broke into a house from the roof, there are five-year-olds who'd know where to go get a gun and shoot him. Hearing that Santa Claus was just one big lie was a huge disappointment for me when I found out—a couple of years ago—and it'll continue to be a downer for future kids unless we do something about it now. I say we take this fat old compulsive giver and shoot him in the head! That's my position: Kill Santa Claus. Does anyone have a problem with that?

• • •

"This country has become fixated on a Santa Claus syndrome. Paul Tsongas ran on the slogan 'I'm not Santa Claus.' Of course, he's not president, either."

• • •

"Remember, Santa only comes once a year. And that's down a chimney."

—Bill

My Dream Panels

People often ask me what my dream panel would be, and I have several, none of which would be what we do on *Politically Incorrect*. On the show, we try as hard as we can to *mis*match people—but in my dreams, I'd like to invite:

• Ringo, Paul, and George, plus their longtime producer, George Martin, just because I'm a Beatles nut, and think I could interview them better than anybody has yet.

• Charles Grodin, Gore Vidal, Joe Queenan, and Fran Lebowitz, just to have one show where I'm perceived as the *fifth* most cynical person on the panel.

• Barbara Carrera, Raquel Welch, Laura Gemser—star of many fine *Emmanuelle* films—and Jennifer Aniston, for obvious reasons—my four favorite celluloid turn-ons, for whom no further justification is needed.

• And two panels of my oldest friends who have all just killed me all the time for the last fifteen years: 1) Jim Vallely, Jerry Seinfeld, Gilbert Gottfried, and Larry Miller; 2) Richard Belzer, Kevin Rooney, Carol Leifer, and Joe Bolster.

I'm working on a list of my favorite politicians, but this may take some time.

About the Author

BILL MAHER is the host and creator of *Politically Incorrect*. He is also a state-of-the-art stand-up comedian.